The Forward Book of Poetry
2026

The Forward Book of Poetry
2026

First published in Great Britain by
Forward Arts Foundation · Somerset House Exchange
The Strand · London · WC2R 1LA
in association with
Faber & Faber Ltd · The Bindery · 51 Hatton Garden · London EC1N 8HN

ISBN 9780571397679 (paperback)

Typeset by Tom Chivers

Printed and bound by CPI Group (UK) · Croydon CR0 4YY

Our authorised representative in the EU for product safety is
Easy Access System Europe, Mustamäe tee 50, 10621 Tallinn, Estonia
gpsr.requests@easproject.com

10 9 8 7 6 5 4 3 2 1

A CIP catalogue reference for this book
is available at the British Library

to Jamie Andrews

Contents

The Forward Prize for Best Single Poem – Performed
Shortlisted poems

The Forward Prize for Best Single Poem – Written
Shortlisted poems

Highly Commended Poems

Foreword

I thought I knew what poetry was. I studied its canon, began my career writing it, and though I left its small-seeming environs promptly for the more expansive-seeming fields of fiction, I've tried to revisit the poetry world as a reader and supporter, and keep a functional – if not fluent – knowledge of its languages. I've said quite often at book events - sighing, as if lorn, as if a little unreconciled – that poetry is still my first love. When I was asked to chair the Forward Prizes, I was reasonably confident I wouldn't be useless to the proceedings. I'd know enough not to sound completely lost – a returning prodigal rather than a crash-landed alien. *Good to have someone neutral chairing from outside the bounds*, the invitation said. So, why not?

It turns out that the depth and breadth of contemporary poetry requires not confidence, but humility, awe and openness; a willingness to be overwhelmed by its incredible, beautiful ecosystems, which grow ever richer and more diverse. Moreover, it requires intrepid and seasoned guides to navigate the pathways. Four were already on hand: Rommi Smith, Lisa Kelly, Hannah Lavery and Sean O'Brien. Sitting round the table for introductions, they seemed like a team of elite athletes or special agents. They were honed, wise, knowledgable, prepared. They'd seen and experienced campaigns, understood successive administrations – from ancient ones through to the current – and supported coups (I speculate). They exuded sagacity, scrutiny and very good energy. They had traversed the estates, the commons and the wilds of poetry, and if there were unfamiliar areas they had the right equipment to explore. *We'll get out of this alive*, I thought.

The first meeting was long and intense. In fact, we overran and had to schedule another. It was long, intense and overrunning not because of differences of opinion and preference – there were those, of course – but because the volume of entries and bodies of work required thoroughness, due given to individual collections, single poems and performances. Poems were considered, critiqued and voiced; their spirit, craftwork, ambition and execution assessed. And because poetry is radical and regenerative, as well as formal and predefined, there were big, seismic discussions about its very nature and identity: the *poetry*-ness of poetry. How might we consider literary history and its future? Politics and the personal? Trends and integrity? How are its enclosures best used, adapted, levelled, rebuilt? How are its languages expressed, translated and made most affective – textually, orally, and, since we were judging a new category, kinetically? Is it fundamentally restricted, shaped and contained, or is it – should it be – unboundaried territory, totally free?

The Forward Prize is unique in its forthright and commendable aim to expand both poetry's remit and its readership – to connect widely with new audiences; to represent the fullest spectrum of art and practice. The fundamental tenet is inclusion, rather than exclusion. This, too, made for challenging debate, because a curatorial role – while not separate from quality control – requires additional bevelling and balance. Proclivities, agendas, misunderstandings, wishes, epiphanies, persuasions, provocations, gives, gains, sympathies, surprises, salvages – all these principles went into the tumbler in the hope of a brilliant final cut.

It occurs to me now that no matter how many additional hours the organisers kindly and patiently allocated us, we could easily have filled them all, with no exit results. But shortlists had to be – and were – made, painfully, rigorously, and (I hope) quite joyfully. Here, again, Mónica Parle and the mighty Forward team must be thanked for firm stewardship, elegance and good grace in corralling our decisions.

Poems from the shortlists feature in these pages, but so too do those we have commended, a selection which was an absolute boon to be able to choose. These really give a sense of the rich interiors of creative traditions, as well as the far shores and outer moons of the contemporary poetry system. It's vital to note that individual poems have the power to become indelible in the mind and memory; to mark our most significant moments in life. Whether celebrating them, symbolising them, lamenting them, or just bearing witness: a poem might provide enough companionship in grief or trauma or isolation that it transforms or saves a life.

So what do we hope this anthology offers? What will the exploratory reader find in these pages?

Together, this writing is virtuosic, spiritual, sensual and humanistic; it is culturally broad and culturally specific; it is global and very local. In the old way, it tells stories – indigenous, colonial, agricultural, urban, inherited, newly invented. It is embodied, but not solipsistic; cerebral and philosophical, yet heart-anchored; truthful, manifest and as undeniable as a mountain or a diamond. It is measured and free-poured, damning and restorative. It is populated not only by humanity, with all humanity's concomitant muck, magic and mindfulness, but also by our human animality – our place in nature and nature's place in us. It is filled with our co-creatures and their environments: elephants, anteaters, caribou, bullfrogs, cockles, butterflies, dogs, foxes (inevitably foxes), plains, tropics, forests, waterways, moors, cities, high-rises, bunkers, craters, oceans and archipelagos.

This poetry recognises our positions, shared spaces, contested histories, broken homes and conflict zones, as well as the inescapable and culpable coordinates of the self. It journeys miles and works multiple occupations; it stays with the children and goes out to look for lost ones. It trespasses where it encounters No-Entry signs, and though it might occasionally sit and enjoy a nice sunset, it will not abide by horizons, but passes over, through, onwards, upwards (fuck the maps – leave a trail of words). It asks for God and sits down with demons. It is confrontational, appeasing, entertaining and diplomatic. It is academic, but rewrites the rules; introduces new conventions of linguistic weighting, mass and meaning. Its innovations and evolutions beguile, amuse and sometimes (rightly) offend. Its architecture is structurally glorious, but can also be deconstructed and transformed; a single stone speaks volumes, or is silenced, or is picked up and thrown. It sings, prays, curses, dreams and choruses.

How foolish ever to have imagined that poetry was small; how wonderful to be reminded that at best it is truly expansive, maximalist, even – and in a single line – universal. It is an art form to which we belong, and always have, and will do more and more, thanks to this prize and these poets. Even if we have travelled away, been seduced by other literature, been made to feel cynical or alienated, or have simply forgotten that poetry is our collective literary habitat, it remains ingathering, and returns us all.

Sarah Hall
Chair of judges
July 2025

Preface

Recently, 51 school pupils gathered in Dagenham, London, as part of a pilot poetry scheme Forward organised. Each poetry club was co-designed with writers, teachers and the young people themselves. The celebrations included an open mic and sharing ideas to incorporate more poetry into their school communities. The students shared how the last six months made them think and feel differently about themselves: "I didn't like poetry at first, but I started doing it because I wanted to try something out of my comfort zone," one shared. "I didn't know I was good at poetry until Miss read my work, and I felt very much inspired."

This was wonderful to hear. But across the UK, knowing how good it feels to write poetry is on the decline. Sobering figures from 2025 research by the National Literacy Trust highlighted a sharp decline in writing for pleasure, from one in two fifteen years ago, to one in four now – a halving of previous rates. But these Dagenham school children? They're now committed poetry activists, with a standout future goal: to recruit more members.

It feels ever more vital that all people get to experience the life-changing benefits of poetry. In an era of seismic cultural, environmental, and technological change, the solace that poetry can provide feels absolutely critical, especially when we consider the current mental health crisis among teens. Poetry is one of the most accessible and low-cost tools for improving mental health and emotional resilience. A 2023 study by the Universities of Plymouth and Nottingham Trent found that 51 per cent of participants who read, wrote, or shared poetry reported reduced feelings of loneliness or isolation, while 50 per cent experienced alleviation of anxiety and depression. Yet poetry remains underutilised as a tool to boost wellbeing and rebuild communities.

In this context, Forward's work feels ever more critical. We are focused on highlighting the tremendous things poetry can do, and helping readers discover its mood-boosting benefits. As Shahidha Bari said in the 2020 anthology, it takes just one poem to turn a reader into a lifelong poetry person. Since I launched this prize in 1992, the Forward team and I have remained focused on breaking down barriers between the poetry corner and the wider world. We are not interested in speaking only to, or on behalf of, the literary establishment. We want to engage with the establishment and beyond. This prize aims to tempt new audiences and show the many varied ways this artform can soar.

You hold in your hand the results: this volume gathers the work of seventy poets, who have published or performed between 2024 and early 2025. These selections were made from more than 500 submissions. We are also publishing for the first time transcripts of the poems shortlisted in the performance category. We have hesitated to do this in the past because we wanted to honour the fact that some poets choose performance over written forms, rather than assuming all poets want to occupy the page, but this year, we have given poets the option to be included, with wonderful results.

This year's best collection shortlistees navigate migration, history, geography, gender and sexuality. Juana Adcock explores cultural transmission across the US/Mexico border and transnational migration, playing with language and form to interrogate violence, gender and inheritance. Leo Boix leads us off on a vast journey across centuries, myths, legends and imagination, using his own experience as a queer, Latinx immigrant from Argentina to chart our understanding of the present against the backdrop of colonialism, the age of explorers and early naturalists, superstition, family and folklore. Niall Campbell draws on folklore, memory, and history to deliver a lyrical meditation on fatherhood, nature and isolation. Vidyan Ravinthiran blends philosophical depth with personal intimacy, interrogating love, race and epistemology in tight, formally inventive poems. Karen Solie delivers witty and sharp commentary on ecological devastation, and finding the sacred and serene in the natural world.

The five books shortlisted for the Jerwood Prize for Best First Collection – by Isabelle Baafi, Sarah Ghazal Ali, Catherine-Esther Cowie, Desree and Michael Mullen – navigate faith, transgenerational heritage, trauma, spirituality and grief. Plus, this year for the first time, the Performed category features poems by Raymond Antrobus and Zoë McWhinney, composed in British Sign Language.

This volume emerged from many hours of considered reading and often intense debate among our judges, who spent months with the 212 volumes of poetry and 308 individual poems. Our deepest thanks to our chair, novelist and two-time winner of the BBC National Short Story

Award Sarah Hall, and fellow judges, poets Lisa Kelly, Hannah Lavery, Sean O'Brien and Rommi Smith, for sharing their time, expertise and passion with each other and us. The consideration and care shown each year in the judging meetings is enough to restore your faith in the poetry community.

Thanks are also due to Jerwood Foundation, which has signed on to support the Prizes for two more years (2025, 2026). As we watch so many of our peer-prizes close, we are so grateful for their support, and, in recognition, we have named the Jerwood Prize for Best First Collection in their honour. We are also grateful to Arts Council England and the John Ellerman Foundation.

Thank you, too, to fellow trustees of the Forward Arts Foundation: Jamie Andrews, our outgoing chair to whom this volume is dedicated, Mary Amanuel, Kim Evans, Aoife O'Connor, Maya Ophelia, Latinka Pilipovic and Amelia Richards.

Thanks to the Forward Arts Foundation's staff: Jay Bhadricha, our Head of Programmes, who shepherds this and our other flagship programme National Poetry Day; and our Co-Executive Directors, Lucy Macnab and Mónica Parle, who have steadied Forward's rudders in a challenging charity climate. Thank you also to the wonderful Tom Chivers, a stalwart poetry champion who brings such humour and know-how to our team each year; and to Kirsten Irving and John Clegg, who moved mountains to help bring this volume together under ridiculously tight time constraints.

William Sieghart
Founder of the Forward Prizes for Poetry
July 2025

The Forward Prize for Best Collection
Selected poems from the shortlisted books

Juana Adcock

In Springfield, Mexico, Lisa Simpson Speaks in Spanish

SCENE I. LISA SIMPSON SPEAKS OF THE DUBBING ACTOR
WHO VOICED HER FOR LATIN AMERICA

Many people don't know this
since I wear pearls round my neck
like an upper-class 1950s North American teen
and my skin is crayoned in an invisible hue
that does not at first glance
appear to signal *meaning*

but for most of my life I was voiced
by Patricia Acevedo Limón.
A career woman in Mexico City
brown eyes, brown skin
bowl haircut, statement jewellery
reminiscent of indigenous cultures.

Despite the success of the show
she never flaunted my name.
Instead she gave interviews
at deserted stalls in obscure
Mexican comic book conventions
did her own housework and rode the bus.

While still very young
she attended a voiceover school
that taught her to make her voice more palatable
to a wider Latin American audience.
How to use neutral words
in an *unmarked* accent

how to push her timbre
to the back of her palatoglossal arch

in the style of the Spaniards
to the edge of her oropharynx
as far back as she could
to furthermost corner of the head

while still revealing a tender emotion
the way women are expected from birth
to take up as little space as possible
even within our own physical structures

**After Banksy (Everybody Wanted to Buy a Plot of
Land in Paradise)**

With the nearest airport just thirty minutes away
the sand was white as sugar the waves
refracted like a precious gem the turtles
could still be swum with

(though now there was a queue)
and the value of property was set to rise
faster than the levels of the ocean
that the city was built to overlook.

Both jungle and holy land as concepts
remained lush. Our parents were rich
and the workplace was changing:
our dreams were no longer remote.

The main square featured
hideous public art
and a pious little chapel
with an altar-fountain

and walls made of heart vines
to make us think of love.
And for the amusement of all
a night market and fair

where some displaced indigenous people
had been granted a permit
to perform their ritual dances
out of season every night

and beg for change

Leo Boix

Sonnet 36

The year after I arrived in England, I became a newsboy.
I had to deliver a Latin American newspaper to London's
Latino restaurants, kiosks and salsa clubs: there was no joy
in that enterprise, and I was happy when it was done.
The van driver was a man from Colombia called Juan,
who was very religious, went to the Charismatic Church
and would pray while driving, and me, well I just yawned.
We would start very early until all addresses were checked.
Then one day, while doing our rounds, he parked the camper,
looked at me and said: *Let's pray together. Here. Right now.*
Think of three wishes, and la virgen purísima *will deliver.*
He closed his eyes and began to pray. I pretended to follow.
Let me stay here in England, and let me be a poet one day.
He started the engine, winked at me, and the van sped away.

Sonnet 74

A long-nose male harlequin frog (*Atelopus longirostrex*)
whistles in the cloud forests of Ecuador's tropical Andes.
Its brown skin with large yellow spots is a cosmic vortex
to attract its near orbiting mate like Saturn to his Tethys.
It keeps still on a mossy rock by a stream, then climbs
to the highest point, a summit, for all dwellers to hear.
Nearby, a group of brown-faced spider monkeys mime
each other while a Chocó toucan sings, then disappears.
The small frog with its pronounced snout calls and calls,
its throat expands, warming the mist clouds that descend
as the place is shrouded in water drops before night falls,
turning the Amazonian forest into a loud choral blend.
I once heard his strange call as a teenager as it got silent.
A song pierced the forest like a foreign tongue, defiant.

Niall Campbell

A Man Carrying His Own Door

Ah yes, the man is at his life again.
Or so I think – when watching him,
prince with his duties, easing nails
from a hinge, the hinge from its grooved wall.

He liked this work. The hammer stroke,
the chisel peeling butter curls
of whitest wood – their pattern fall
around the job's circumference.

And now it's lifted free – hauled free
into the air – just like those tenants,
who, once evicted, since wood was rare,
were free to take their doors with them.

Can't you see it? The huge shield-weight
of a door being carried by a man.
Near seventy, now. But just you try
to share the weight, or take an end.

Oblivion – or something softer
and just as dark has said its name.
The rain is knocking, hard as light,
where he holds the wood beside his ear.

The Cockle-picker

He lifts the notch of shell, small cup,
our thimble of the sea's champagne,
our muscle drink, the flesh-downed taste.
Worlds off from wine, and what wine toasts.

Low tide, the beckon clouds all out,
the cockle shells raked fresh; hands prising
their groove-cut, pearl-white cask. He savours,
same as I do, this coastal life.

Vidyan Ravinthiran

Autumn

after John Keats

The fallen yellow leaves now oftener
flare red. Embers. Blown-up chilli flakes.
The burning of the library at Jaffna.
Foreign dead about to break
the spell of here and now. Phantasms steal
into the peaceful lives we seem to have earned,
telling tales about what happened
to them, not us, and in a tongue I never learned.
This is my garden, my spade of blood meal
and from our kitchen the time-travelling smell
of chicken curry floats to Walden Pond.

—A swooping cardinal like a struck match.
Above the fence mosquitoes eddy
like opinion, crazed by a patch
of red-pink light into giddy
scribbling on the air. There is no need
to be ashamed. I see you there and keep
alive the thought of meeting one day
brightly after the next. Black mustard seed
thrums in the sauce, the sky falls asleep;
where feelings come from or may leap
across and through and to no one can say.

Tsunami-hit, shoved over at a tilt,
they've left the bashed old kovil's god-thronged tower
standing, tallish, beyond the new one built
to face, this time, becalm, the ocean's power...
Our autumn clouds are a far-quarried rubble
to which the changing light does spicy things.

To sing, to fly, migrate, are curious verbs;
beauty, like happiness, frailly reliable,
has nothing to do with why there are wings,
why birds build nests and sing their songs,
or why barbed wire's besotted with its barbs.

As a child

because my voice was not the right voice
and could not be understood I stood
before the *mirror* – a murky glassen word
this mouth can't shape right to this day – and was made
to watch my teeth and lips being imprecise.
So this is why I come across a Southron
and not from Yorkshire, or Sri Lankan; but I'll complain
no more about this clarified and potent tongue

for when the moustached gent at US Customs
asked me in his hapless twang
are you a terrorist, my borrowed posh it sure
abashed that poor colonial; and it was of course
what my child-face perceived or could not in the glass
which made of me a scrutineer of sound,
a listener for and into every glitch
in the aathma, the script, the avid void of English.

Karen Solie

That Which Was Learned in Youth Is Always Most Familiar

for Erik

Returning from a walk through the fields
in the dirty realism of early spring,
he ran up beside me and said *Auntie,*
do you know what? And I said *What,*

    expecting a load of nonsense about cartoons,
    trucks, the dog, or the recitation
    of a poorly communicated half truth
    misheard in school, having never believed children possess

      an essential knowledge or intuition
      that age, like water, like wind, erodes,
      in ignorance recast as innocence
      by all the insipid diocese of wellness

        in spite of the very obvious reasons
        our factory settings are reprogrammed,
        and the sooner the better, actually,
        I've been a child –

    But he said *Auntie, I think there are two kinds of shapes.*
    Replaceable and irreplaceable shapes.
    Triangles, circles, squares, we can make them. But this
    – he held a clod of earth –

is an accident. Will never happen again.
He threw it to the gravel
where it shattered in a rhetorical flourish
of one example made various

and each, he promised, singular.
He's five. And not even I,
who would sooner be right than happy,
could argue.

Red Spring

Turbulence over the prairie in May, heat rising

from the just-sown fields. Warmth has unbound the soil,

and from above, lakes, rivers, sloughs

appear as holes in the cloth of settlement, and another world

at play underneath, where *no colonist*

Mastered the wild earth; no land was marked, none parcelled out,

runoff sparkling in the ditches if the snow

fell this year, no joy in winter without snow, no joy

in spring. Through last year's chem fallow, the first raw

leaves unfold, the infant snub-nosed coleoptile

climbs from the cradle of the GMO seed patent,

the earliest stage at which herbicides

may be applied – Luxxur™ for problematic grass weeds –

as white-tailed fawns sleep inside wild chokecherry

in hollowed-out rooms a man can stand up in.

Ask at the mansions of the skies

for rain, and at the all-important tillering stage

apply fertilizer, insecticide, Buctril M™

to which there is no confirmed resistance in Canada, Infinity FX™

for chem-resistant volunteers.

By the power of Bayer (née Monsanto), the chemical

is wedded to the seed. They are literally

made for each other. There is no going back. Yet still

nature lurks within the soil

and the weeds jump up unbidden, each year a little smarter

and more vigorous, with the high-pitched optimism

of adaptation, sinking their anchors into the deep

and banging their empty cups on the table

– foxtail, cleavers, sow thistle, kochia –

and new beetles arrive from the south with their briefcases,

new viruses, fusarium head blight

against which are deployed the foliar fungicides

– Prosaro™, Folicur™ –

and at booting the critical growth regulators

as crop insurance yield-loss coverage begins

lest the scant moisture fail the barren sands

at the very emergence of inflorescence, a delicate phase prone

to environmental stress, aren't we all,

full of oil, blood, systemic glyphosate

advertised as non-persistent; but tell that to DeWayne Johnson

and his non-Hodgkin lymphoma,

ask the crew boss who cleared the nozzle of my sprayer

by blowing through it, they can't go back.

I was given no mask and threw up for six hours.

So strong is custom formed in early years.

I'm sorry, I can't make this beautiful.

Bayer (and formerly Monsanto) admits no wrongdoing,

even with 9.6 billion reserved to settle

pending litigation, another 1.25 to address

future litigation, its proprietary gene technology whispering

in the ears of grain ripening through

its early, middle, and late milks. The chemical

in the field respects the gene, and the farmer the authority

of Bayer (and formerly of Monsanto)

who will not hesitate to make of you an example

if you insult its canola patent by growing your own seed.

Such wide confusion fills the countryside,

it's said you can't go back. Unless you're rich enough

to farm years at a loss, you can't. Corporations buy the land

of those who die or move, and so assembles the hidden machinery of our lives: the feedlots, gas wells, sweatshops, coal mines.

We don't like to think too much about it –

Bayer in our kitchens, in our bread,

as we are its kitchen, the heart of its home, and if we can afford

a nine-dollar loaf of artisan organic ancient grain sourdough

it lives in us too because of those who cannot. When in

its grey facilities, Bayer (and formerly Monsanto)

engineers its terminator seeds, suicide seeds

of a zombie technology, a plant more dead than alive,

and when it patents what it promises not to use, do we believe it?

Can we go back? Meet each other in the old knowledge?

I don't know how to make this beautiful,

though when the wind trails its fingers through the durum

it is, and a day's work is measurable by the eye,

when antelope walk the hills at dusk like grass-fed spirits

from the otherworld, before the grid,

when the ancient science of a cover crop of yellow sweet clover

or alfalfa sings into the air a fragrance

drawing to itself the fragile pollinators,

butterflies, ladybugs, and the bees to their harvest –

the colony come forth to sport and play

so deep their love of flowers –

it's beautiful, when sleeping populations open their eyes

and nitrogen is fixed inside the earth.

Jerwood Prize for Best First Collection
Selected poems from the shortlisted books

Sarah Ghazal Ali

Story of the Cranes

١

A young girl with a face full of eyes asks her baba,

Baba, do you know
everything?

Baba tells her he knows everything.

Through seeping eyes, lies appear
feathered with truth.

She offers him a red book
from the shelf with another question.

Baba tells her *The Satanic Verses* is a secret God
kept from us, stories Shaytan wasn't allowed to share,
Poor Shaytan.

Shouldn't he get to tell his side of things?

Baba points out the window.
Shaytan wants us to worship the birds.

Baba knows cranes fly with necks elongated.
That there were three beautiful and beloved long ago.
He knows their names in Farsi, in Urdu.

But in Arabic – *al-Gharaniq* الغرانيق
This she learned on her own.

Baba installs a birdbath.
So the cranes might bless us with their presence!

Baba goes birdwatching.
God is here, around us, not above!

At the park, her eyes shutter if Baba comes too close.
He always pushes the swing too high.

٢

Birds flood my dreams,
fill the night and cut me.

I memorized the names of every human
bone, shoulder to finger, to stay awake.
Despite my best efforts, I'd drift off, always
waking with shoulders sore, phantom

pain reminding me what my body was not
made for.

What was my body made for?

٣

Today, two colorless birds drag
their shadows across the grass.

I imagine looping wire thread around their bodies,
tossing them into the air like broken kites.
It's too easy to be cruel now.

I demonstrate to the creatures in audience
my full and human length. How high
I can stretch, arms breaching their sky.

٤

God addresses the three cranes by name,

devotes two of sixty-two verses to this end.

I imagine the young girl in audience as the Prophet
stands to echo this surah to a crowd.

I see her child eyes,
how easily they reveal their want.

> I learned on my own
> that when he finished speaking,
> believers and nonbelievers alike fell to their knees,
> so affected were they by the answers
> to questions no one knew to ask.

I see her falling with the best of them, devotion rippling
across her face.

o

In the mirror, the wrong eyes run down my face.

*Baba, do you know
everything?*

Baba smiles
and shows me his long neck.

The Guest

I heard his knock in the corridors of sleep
and woke to let him in.

Imagine my heart in my feet
as I stepped out of bed and over a snake

that darted away so fast I doubted my eyes,
whether it really grazed my ankle

or if my sight convinced me
of some artificial touch –

all the dramatics of a retina
eager to spin brightness from a long night.

I am trying not to conflate
snakes with the first garden,

trying not to fixate on capacity,
on travelers morphing into conquerors

but patterns becoming means
for celestial navigation,

trying to focus on the guest, patient,
waiting behind a door.

The Bedouins dubbed him
        Tariq – a morning star
          mapping the sand of a dream.

There was a room – I touched its walls.
A figure – his knock rustled behind my eyes.

There was a diaphanous scene leaking
through the gap under my door.

I blamed the trees for their wood, I wondered
if he was tired from walking. If the grass

constellated beneath him. If his eyes darkened
with the night. I press hard against mine.

Isabelle Baafi

Anti-Hero

You said you saw me through the crowd
and imagined rummaging through my hair.

Said you heard my laugh through walls
and could tell my fillings were made of gold.

My pixels make your pixels spasm.
I'm still not sure why.

When you ask me my favourite colour,
I send an encrypted file

from a laptop with no password.
The file cannot be opened because there are problems with the contents.

The file was copied and pasted
from a traumatised motherboard.

But you eat the rice I burned so I'll know
I am not too hard to stomach. Asking to touch

the dry patch I leave on a bench after sitting
in the rain. Wanting me to confide that once

I followed a snail to its nest
and drowned its eggs because they looked happy.

Once, I climbed a bell tower
and burned the rope with a mirror and the sun.

You tell me that your first job was
installing peepholes that worked both ways.

But the locals chased the inventor out of town
when the streets became full of suspicious couples

staring at each other's eyeballs for days.
Sometimes, I think it's for password clues that you ask

who taught me to ride a bike.
Why I buy so much bubble wrap.

Where I was when the last po'ouli died.
How I calm a memory when it's plucked.

Sometimes, I scratch the mole on my scalp
that you found when you washed my hair.

The parts of me that I only know exist
because you saw them.

The Butterfly Effect

A phenomenon in which a minute change in one context can have huge effects elsewhere

13

Am I root or stem? Changing
ways: scarred and new in growing.
Remember
a tide carving its future. Your
whole mind splintered,
rogue all summer. That and
scorching Blackpool, and
the donkey panting on heavy legs. My
mother – watching waves,
but drinks nothing.
Am I
learning thirst?
My fatherly frown,
my remnant
of him in retrograde.
Course of coarse.
Reclaiming shells, gleaning
dust and bone. Armour discarded.
Afterlife: twisting, surging. Am I
my past?
I regret hardening.
Nothing left
behind.

31

Changing stem or root? I am
growing in new and scarred ways.
Remember
your future, its carving tide. A
splintered mind, whole.
And that summer: all rogue.
And Blackpool scorching,
my legs heavy on panting donkey, the
waves watching Mother.
Nothing drinks. But
I am
thirst, learning.
Frown fatherly, my
remnant; my
retrograde in him. Of
coarse, of course.
Gleaning shells, reclaiming
discarded armour – bone and dust.
I am surging, twisting afterlife
past my
hardening regret. I
left nothing
behind.

Catherine-Esther Cowie

Mimorian

after Carlos Drummond's 'Resíduo'

Only a little of me remains, a fixture,
Madwoman locked in a downstairs room,
four-walled gag, muffler. Of my ravings,
the upstairs hear nothing, nothing.
But still a little of me will stay, the stink of me
in the sheets, on the walls, on their tongues,
wagging, wagging all night long about
my bad romances – chupid woman,
sad woman
                object lesson.

Of my illness, they talk too much,
I am spectacle, spectre, fire-lover
wandering off into the bush, the market square.
My early morning peep shows, the breaking
day, someone forgot to lock my room, again,
the music loud in my head, how I shook,
shook the neighbourhood awake with my naked breasts,
my grandchildren cried, their friends can't come over.
And of those things I remember
so little
      so little
why can't they *do* the same?

Of the things I enjoy,
they won't remember, the mourning doves
nesting in the monstrous breadfruit tree,
rum thrown back, going deep
down, deep down between my legs,
my hair brushed and slick and smoothed
into a bun, my yellow satin ribbon.

Of God, am I against, for
or indifferent, they've never asked
or cared to know. My mother,
father, their names...
already they've forgotten.
Of my love of white, they'll remember
cotton dresses bleached in a blinding sun,
my men, always, always fair.

Of me so little will remain, stripped
and pared down to a fear,
bright and blossoming in the back
of a young girl's head: ou fou ou fou
ou fou

        ou fou.

What I Know

'Men are threatening presences.'
– *Lucy Ellmann*

I.

    St Lucia, 1950

I hit Auntie in the face.
She tried to sell my sisters.
I hit her again. We hid.
The spoon was wooden,
broke Auntie's nose.
She said our mother wasn't coming back.
She said tourists love mixed girls,
I was too old.
I told my sisters, if Auntie finds us,
brings them to a big white ship,
remember, our mother is the sea,
jump.

II.

    St Lucia, 1990

I hit my daughter. Even now,
she throws the past at me,
some sports uniform I burnt
when she was thirteen.
Netball, she says, netball.
She came home after five.
What did she expect? I cuffed her ear
when she refused to undress.
Yes, the sun was only beginning to set,
yes, she barely had breasts.
But when had that ever put them off?
You stopped me from being me, she cries.
I tell her, this is what I know,
my hands staving off men.

Desree

The Notorious B.I.G. and Jesus Christ on a Boat

Then, without warning, a furious storm came.
Billows big enough to separate the weak from the
obsolete. Biggie sucks saliva from behind his teeth, throws
his hands in da air and Jesus sighs. Waves permeate the
cleats of the boat, like bullets, and drive by.

Sweat dances down Biggie's cheek. Finally,
Jesus asks *Why are you so afraid?* Biggie pats his wallet to
check his pride is still there; he wants forgiveness, but
Jesus too has cast out all that sold and bought on his
block.

*There is no greater love than this – that a man
should lay down his life for his friends.* Biggie shifts from
the stern to the gunwale. The boat does not falter. Jesus
takes out a crustless tuna sandwich, pulls it apart from the
middle, hands half to Biggie. They chew watching the
waves turn to foam as the sky hums a perfect blue.

Kim K Takes a Photo of Sarah Baartman to Her Surgeon

The surgeon nods,
scarifies a note
or two, captures
a photo. Studies
Sarah's ass, looks
for a scar left from
an incision. Kim coughs. Sighs.
Asks if he can do what God did
not. Pilfer the 'hot' from Hottentot.
Give her that slim, thique, steatopygic
silhouette. 'I want to be the number
one freak at this show. I want people
to wonder about my origins. Get
me a tight fitted garment, a
crowd and I will give
you just enough, so it
looks like consent'.

Michael Mullen

He Loved Lilies

Their spooky white, the flab of their pinched buds.
He filled the house with them when he quit drinking.
Loved their burst alien jaws, the spiced odour
of their breath. His mother couldn't hack them,
said they stank of death. He loved lilies,
their mole-nosed bloom.
He told me he liked me because I looked boyish.
He loved lilies, fat fleshy stars
amongst the sheen of leaves. Emitting migraines
from their linen maws. He loved lilies –
they look adult. Their white-green stipple,
vasefuls of split phalli, they go well with the walls.
He loved lilies, the ginger rust
of their shrunken almonds, lightly spiked,
the bruise-barbed throat.
He would sniff them when we were done.
He loved lilies. Let them wilt
till their lines looked like a tea-stained Schiele.
He loved lilies. The decay of perfume's
heady mould. I don't say much.
He never asked for a poem. He loved lilies
to touch – part skin, part climax. An encased pond
of jilted fireworks – frozen flares. He loved lilies.
He told everyone. He took photos of them
in blank light. He loved lilies. Their inverted fans. Their
bent wings. Their beauty – ghostly and mute.

Tinamints

Rid firmamints – jostlin the skyline
Atlas-backed manses cerryin dreich.
Trickin yir eye – wae each bent windae – burnt shooders
skimmin smirr – sittin squat. Tabacca shadet tinamints
windaes riflectin sun rages. Indipindint
stawnin oan eez tod – great survivor ae renovations.
Klimt-licht, ginger brick, a solid frieze of mason's origami
gutter linet, lit lang sketches alang eez surface.
Pirmanint – they press doon the highstreets – hawf hexagon
is the sandstone brow ae yer favourite drinkin establishment.
Blonde constant. Lissun how sonorous yer words ae
longing – jaunt to the close – bellowin doon the sliver
ae solid livin. Yer consonants trapped
in its algae-patched grimace or skittin on
the line-gilded tiles of a wally close in shades ae
cheerie rid ur gaulden snooty. Steamboat puffs addin
their ane glamour, as if these behemoths could undock
n sail the street. Lives stacked on each othir
lit stanzas – glawin amber caverns – monstera hands
clasped oantae windaes. Whit lives these tenements huv cooried,
terracotta pots shorn tae a tapestry ae jawlines,
rain-drenched each year n yet they breathe
sparkle-dry – peat-broon bruise, blue shade
made livin light. Fuck yer tombstones – when I go
tell them I was powdered tae dust n mixed
wae Scotland's best brick – ma eulogy –
Hail thi stane thit hames us.

The Forward Prize for Best Single Poem –
Performed
Shortlisted poems

Scan the QR code to watch the shortlisted poems

Raymond Antrobus

Dynamic Disks, 1933

My phone memory is full
of canvases I have cried in front of –
circles, holes –
Shadows on water.

——

There was a point
you wanted to stay
but couldn't stop
floating in the air.
The sight of you
is a thing
I keep orbiting.
I was afraid
of rejection –
knew I'd give it
too much meaning,
or not enough.

——

Sat in the glossy Guggenheim gallery,
eyes on Kupka's *Dynamic Disks*,
I began to think of relationships as circles,
the blue/red/white/black spirals imperfect
and un-unioned, obscuring the broken run
of black lines, the way
they break
like eggs, waves, light bulbs, marriages.
Since our separation I have been spilling
ink on lined pages, wondering what stopped
working when the plates were put away and
how many times we asked with water in our eyes
what we wanted if it wasn't art on the wall
in the house by the sea?

Bella Cox

Sikiliza

i)

July is baking this London balcony // Barcelona beach // Nairobi jacaranda-lined street // to sweltering // parked outside Johannesburg's Market Theatre // a London ambulance wailing // you hear 'Vuli Ndlela' playing // someone swears in French // you are circling Geneva's three-legged chair // on Westlands roundabout a street kid named Moses begs for *mandazi* money // Oyster card ready // a shirtless man calls you *guapísima* // onions and *boerewors* sizzling // the next train will arrive in 2 minutes // you bata for a Maasai necklace // two kites swoop to seize your samosa // you swear in English // your friends are laughing in a nearby pub // tavern // *chiringuito* // there is always beer // the road is long and grey // to the left a sudden wall // red graffiti scrawl // 'You Are Here'

ii)

Here is anywhere you do not wish to be.
You ache for the scent of jasmine every day
until you have it, and then it's mosquitos
that bite you back into yearning for
silly Western things like app-dialled food
deliveries, fast internet speeds.
Your mother wears
her emigrations like medallions,
tells you gratitude is the key
to happy. Her voice,
same resonant hum as honey,
thrums in seven languages.

iii)

You aren't fluent / but / your tongue puzzles itself across three languages / ~~friends' audio notes~~ *les notes audio de tes amis* on repeat / a patchwork of comfort accents / ~~No matter~~ *No importa* where you are / home, ~~is not here~~ *sio hapa* / 'Permanent settlement' ~~does not exist~~ *n'existe pas* / You are accustomed to being ~~misunderstood~~ *incomprendida* / even choosing a binary sexuality feels like choosing ~~one home~~ *nyumba moja* / choosing one home feels like losing another / but you learn / ~~you are learning~~ *unajifunza* to ~~name your body home~~ *llamas a tu cuerpo hogar* / Treat its many sensitivities as ~~sacred~~ *sacrée* / anoint the walls of your skin with ~~coconut oil~~ *mafuta ya nazi* / make it ritual / learn ~~your body's language~~ *le langage de ton corps* / ~~listen~~ *sikiliza* for your gut / pay ~~attention~~ *atención* to your blood / become cartographer of your many states / ~~move to your own winds~~ *bougez à votre guise* / ~~Here~~ *Hapa* you are all that you need / ~~Here you can build~~ *aquí puedes construir* your own mosaic / ~~Here~~ *Ici* you need not / speak

Griot Gabriel

Where I'm From

I'm from a place where poor boys worship rich men.
I'm from a place where we pull wheelies on bikes,
two-wheeling black wheelie bins at night for bin men.

I'm from...
smells of haze
and dogs that bark at starry nights.
I'm from a place where they try to gently gentrify.

I'm from broken men
that write stories with broken pens.

I'm from a perfect God that uses broken men
to tell stories written by their broken pens.

I'm from a place where
the new Nisa Local will forever be called Charlie's.
Because before Nisa became local it was Charlie that would
    charge me.

I'm from bookies on every street corner.
I'm from a place where we have prodigal sons
because we first had prodigal fathers.

I'm from a place where
mums' wrinkled hands join in violent prayer.
I'm from a place where Grand Theft Auto was idolised
by infant eyes
from the days of PS2 to PS5.

I'm from a mother's teary eyes.
I'm from a place where grand juries find joy
in giving judgement to black boys

with crooked laws like joint enterprise.

I'm from...
I tried to carry Mother's pain.

I'm from...
I'm my brother's keeper
so when I win, that's my brother's gain.

I'm from a place where we either have red bloodshot skies
or a blue moon, depending on the score on derby day.

I'm from a place where prophets aren't accepted in their home-
    town
so they have to leave because it hurts to stay.

I'm from a place where we hate to see the feds call.
I love my city,
though it's gritty,
full of nitties.
It's so peak in Piccadilly
cos the rent's tall.

I'm from a place where if your friend dies,
they say you must ride.
I'm from gang wars between Longsight and Moss Side.

I'm from...
empty fridge
and empty belly.
I'm from hangers as aerials
to find signal on the telly.

I'm from poverty.
I'm from hood up means
please don't bother me.

I'm from MMU and Uni of.
I'm from damaged petals on roses
but they don't see the beauty of.

I'm from Adventure and Powerhouse.
I'm from my mum screaming,
'Go charge the electricity before the power's out.'

I'm from a place where
we set the usual urban scene.
I'm from a place where there's an urban youth
from the inner city, and he's got urban dreams.

I'm from a place where he's been moulded by every burden his
    postcode schemes.
I'm from a place nicknamed 'L. A.'. My postcode's M13.

I'm from chiselled yet dishevelled men.
I'm from a bag of man wearing man bags.

I'm from a place where it's face in dirt and handcuffs.
I'm from a place where we sell white flakes like dandruff.

I'm from 'Stop resisting.'
I'm from a place where 'Stop resisting.'
is a metaphor for, 'I wish you'd just stop living.'

I'm from Magnums and spliffs.
I'm from handguns and shifting gears to drift.

I'm from a place where we don't mess with the southern borders.
I'm from a place where you can see a whole new world when you
    enter Northern Quarter.

I'm from 'Where you from bro?'
I'm from 'You dun know the dun know.'

I'm from 'Can anything good come from where I'm from?'
I'm from 'I don't care what you think, I love where I'm from.'

I'm from a place where they scream '0161.'
I'm from a place where everyone's a walking contradiction.

I'm from...
you know where I'm from.

Joshua Idehen

The World According to Your Mum Doing the Washing

Capitalism:
Your mum does the washing. You pay her a dollar. You get her to do your mate's washing. Your mate pays you $50.

Communism:
Your mum does the washing. You do the washing. Every night you salute a photo of your dad.

Socialism:
Your mum does the washing. You do the cooking. Everybody is happy in theory.

Feudalism:
Your mum does the washing and pays you tax.

Colonialism:
You barge into Mum's room. Claim you 'discovered' her room. Dump your dirty clothes on the floor.

Fascism:
Your mum does the washing and you are obsessed with her nose.

Liberalism:
You watch your mum do the washing and feel really really bad. 'Something must be done,' you say. Something may or may not get done.

Libertarianism:
Your mum does the washing. You believe you did the washing.

Religion:
Your mum does the washing. You thank God.

Atheism:
Your mum does the washing. You make a twelve-part YouTube video demanding peer-reviewed evidence that she did, in fact, do the washing.

Americanism:
Your mum does the washing. It's in the Constitution. END OF DISCUSSION.

Mansplaining:
Your mum does the washing. You tell her how best to do the washing. You have never done the washing.

Same-sex marriage:
Your mums do the washing.

Patriarchy:
Your mum doesn't exist. The washing is mysteriously done.

TERFism:
Your mum doesn't want your other mum doing the washing, because of genitals and stuff.

Polling:
There's a 70% chance you will do the washing on Saturday night. Come Sunday morning, it has 100% been done by your mum.

Africanism:
You go to Benny's house. Benny's mum does the washing. You ask your mum, *Why don't you do the washing?* You do not survive the night.

Feminism:
Your mum insists you grow up and do your own washing.

White feminism:
Your mum hires a woman of colour to do the washing.

Male feminism:
That one time I did the washing, I told everyone about it and I blogged about it, bragged about it, took a selfie, Insta story, went on Oprah, won an Oscar, went on *Fortnite*, did a dance. I am an ally. #metoo

Misogyny:
You hate your mum whether or not she does the washing.

Matriarchy:
Your mum does the washing. You do the cooking. You are really happy pulling your weight in the house.

Egalitarianism:
That one time I did the washing is proof everything is equal now and no one needs feminism any more.

Hip Hop:
Every day I'm hustling/ every day I'm hustling/ when I bring the basket/ mama put the washing in.

Narcissism:
You look good in the clothes your mum washed.

Surrealism:
The washing does your mum.

Zoë McWhinney

The Portrait and the Skylight

a joyful, glistening body of water.

A petal-tickled maiden,
One petal plucked and pirouetted away, 'ihy',
Another plucked, pirouette, 'ily'.

Cut to the shadowy crown of a head emerging from the sun lit
   water.

There was a room, ceiling and floor plain as the walls.
Sun's rays narrowing to a close through the skylight as it melts
   into the horizon.
A table and its legs,
Resting upon it, a pot of brushes,
Easel with a canvas standing at a slant.

There, by a thousand brush strokes and smears, is a woman
   floating in water, surrounded by
flowers, and her feeble hands.
The petal arrived and became the painter's brush.
He puts the brush aside in that pot, twiddling his moustache,
   examining his work. And he walked
away, left the room, bop.

A droplet plop. Leak down the canvas.
The skylight above had a little crack growing.
Drip.

Cut to a darkened sky, punctured only by one bright moon
   witnessing

From afar the head rising above, drenched, inhaling –

the skylight, that crack suddenly had branches and these branches
    their own branches, it
spreads across the glass until the glass gave way, burst.

Water slamming down

Roaring along the wall

Splaying there

Rushing to over there

Sweeping the floor

Tackling the table's prongs, tipping the pot spilling the brushes
    painting lands on water, being washed.

But a hand reached out from ether and held onto a petal in the
    painting – plucked it.
Released it so it could dance,
pirouetted up and up to
join the rank of petals on a girl's favourite daisy flower

Her dad, the decorated general, padded shoulders and sash and
    all.
He looked out of the curtains.
A fatality.
The knife point drips heavy with his blood.
It lands, making a crown as her daisy was torn open in grief.

A dark sky, only the watchful moon,
A figure paddling through the water.

A circle of petals but they are of speared metal.
The killer's crown, hand bloodied he stands accuse –

suddenly standing knee deep in the water, gasping,
her wet body started shivering so bad.
Skin detected some warmth, looked but she's blinded by the
    rising Sun.
There's a bird, almost floating in front of her.
A feather falls, it glided to join the water lily's petals, blooming
    one by one until the water is
decorated with floating white and green dots.

The sun affirms, there is forgiveness.

The Forward Prize for Best Single Poem –
Written
Shortlisted poems

Abeer Ameer

at least

it is said/ that they died/ in their sleep/ one might imagine/ a
peaceful state/ at least/ at least/ the moment the skies fell/ on
their small bodies/ and the ground beneath/ crumbled/ at least/
they were asleep/ or at least/ they were in their beds/ maybe verses
of solace/ were recited/ just before/ just before/ they drifted off/
maybe/ lullabies were sung/ to mask/ the sound/

or at least/ they were used to the sound/ it was probably/
background noise/ to them/ white noise/ because of their
backgrounds/ their ground/ so used to it/ for most of their short
lives/ it is said/ that they died in their sleep/ at least/ it was dark/
at least/ they won't have seen/ the rockets/ the rockets signed by
the senders/ at least/ they won't have seen/ the signatures/

at least/ it was night-time/ a single airstrike/ at least/ at least/ in
their last moments/ their souls/ had already left their bodies/ to
the air of dreams/ the unseen land/ a place in hiding/ when eyes
are open/ at least/

at least/ they were drowsy/ or at least/ not fully awake/ at least if
they startled/ it would have been quick/ or at least/ if slow/ they
were floating/ into a dreamy transition/ to the next world/

at least/ now they're just waiting/ for a proper burial/ at least/
at least/ it's over now/ at least/ for the dead/
at least/ these children/ don't need to fear the dark/
at least/ not anymore/

Tom Branfoot

A Parliament of Jets

if I die, I worked for Palestine – and I worked for the birds
– Saed Shomaly

between mountain pines   prickly pears
the River Jordan   and
                                        Mediterranean Sea
olive-rooted hillsides   and military
                checkpoints
each spring
                        millions of migratory
   birds fly over the occupied territories   of Palestine
where settler violence
                                        soars under the state's
                armoured wing

   unwavering naturalists
        and birders risk
        detention   and brutalisation
                        to document
   the visitation
   of swifts

        anyone spotted   with a camera or binoculars
awaits questioning

                only drones are permitted
                        optical advantage

                one risks existence
   to witness
                        a kestrel return
to its nest in the West Bank's limestone cliffs

    for daring to understand
                     life outside
its immediate context   of devastation

              *

low-flying   American-made jets
    rupture atmosphere
                    rumbling over fells
at regular intervals   shoving thunder
        into ears   over-thrust cotton buds

     disarming engines
to barrel-roll over pikes
           superseding buzzards
and other raptors
       in preparation
   for a future war

   in Elterwater   a lone jay swoops
through mossy enclaves
     there is more spilled blood
 in Gaza
than drinking water
         where native sunbirds
   whet scimitars on ambivalent light

no snipers
     scope out our white bodies
       resisting soil and air
  in this recreational   environment

           constructed and purchased
by Englishmen
      to preserve national identity

though rivers   fields and moorland
   are dry-stone enclosed
      allotting authorised strips
                              of managed land
through which to ramble
                        with a semblance
of sublimity

I walk queasy with Romanticism
   below   the military-industrial
complex mimicking avian flight

*

Types of aircraft   that may be seen in the area include
   F-15 Eagle   Typhoon FGR4   Hawk T. 2
   Hercules   and helicopters

         semantic damage   naming combat aircraft
after birds   a predatory metaphor
                        the F-15 Eagle
            boasting hundreds of victories
      in aerial warfare
   with the majority of kills
                  claimed by the Israeli Air Force

                        more aircraft
   have been totalled   by collisions with white storks
         pelicans and other large birds
   gliding over settlements
                     than through enemy conflict

         empires indulge   in hands-free massacres
alienated   from ground blood

                    to enjoy this aerial display
          without cowering in ruins   or a *designated*
safe zone

                                   is a privilege

                 where sound signals nothing
but precision in the colonial sky

    under which a farmer leaves   his pasture
        to inform us
                      of the next Hercules flyover
and not to bawl trespass   red as fresh steak

                              *

no   one   is free
     but

                        some
     are less
       free

                  than others

cleaving valley air for insects   these swifts and swallows
       likely passed
                        through Palestine
        on migration
      from wintering grounds in Africa
                      to European breeding grounds
         excreting amputated memories
  midair

                              trauma transported like a parasite
on the wing

I don't see that there should be separate words
for politics and nature

                                        after Chernobyl
                    Brits were discouraged
          from drinking water from rivers
                              ghylls and tarns

              Ukrainian clouds
          absorbed radiation
                                    before shifting to glide
          over our island
                              raining unknowables and acid
            into open water

of Cumbrian radiation
                    only 50%
                    came from Chernobyl

the rest   blossoming from nuclear
bomb testing
                    the Windscale Fire of 1957
and routine discharges
                              from Windscale   now Sellafield
in the 1960s   and 70s

local and global intersect
overlap   in landscape
                              double exposures

                    still circulating blood
                warmed in flight
                over the West Bank
            a complication of chiffchaff

nestle in wooded tracts

whittled by colonial wealth

*

we hear the same discursive boom of the F-15
between the Langdale Pikes
                              as echo above civilians
               in the largest open-air prison
reduced to collateral
                                        in the *everywhere war*
despite which migration hasn't halted

               birds still visit
     the occupied territories
                                             instilling hope
to the displaced
                    though they become   harder
     to observe
          new checkpoints   roadblocks
and gates in the West Bank

          this is not just a country of war

birdwatching   a counterpoint to death
                         bombings and killings
finch-glimpse of normality

*

F- 1 5   *E a   g le   Ea se*

     d a   l e   I s r   a e l La n   g   d   a   l e

E   a   s

    g   l   e   I   L a
                                                n   g   e   l
                    E   a   I s   r
            s   d   a
                    l   e

R   e   a   l   F-   E   a
d   1 5
        s   d   a   l   e   n   g   l

L

        a   n   g   e   a

                                                s   d

        r   g l F-   1   5   F a   l

a   s   t   i   n

*

relentless aerial bombing

    and military ground invasions

    by Israeli forces have

mutilated

Gazan ecosystems

   and natural

environments

     imperial ecocide

 settlers burning agricultural land

    ancient olive trees

         and Palestinian crops

     white phosphorus in the soil

  the environment a victim

    contaminated with munitions

and toxins

     we are so close to this

  unspeakable

atrocity

    through screens

  swifts

      and fighter jets

 their war-reminding presence

     between the ridges of scars

in the fantasy of wilderness

                    that other place

whirling inside my cortex

                    underneath

this place

        a Geiger counter

chorusing radiation's ghost

        I can hardly breathe in the hush

green air

                    dry stone walls and hedgerows

are the stories we tell

                    of the rural

        visible patterns of ownership

        and usage etched

into the landscape

        checkpoints for marked subjects

we can't imagine   land outside that context

a failing empire   outviolences its past

*

here in the land of teasels   touch-me-not balsam
      and foxgloves

            binoculars   aimed at this hedged blackcap
like a Thing at rest   stress balm
chirping   with its *inly-muttered voice*

      before flying
away
            without a threat of contrails   or noise

Tim Tim Cheng

Girl Ghosts

say Surabaya. Sound like eight again. Girl ghosts pick and choose their countries. Yes to father's nose, mother's eyes. No to her wiggling pair of lí zi, her widowed, high-pitched *lăo lĭ, lăo lĭ*. Girl ghosts beat each other into meat floss. Shout *luun daak*, the only Hokkien girl ghosts pass on. Be it Surabaya or Putien, girl ghosts are rich, beautiful, in denial. Love being loved by landlord fathers. Steam thin rice cakes when the rice runs out. Charge neighbours for watching their TV. Girl ghosts are crying. Girl ghosts are not crying. Girl ghosts are learning èrhú in Fuzhou. Hands, frost-bitten, out of tune. The èrhú cries out for girl ghosts with long faces, low registers. Girl ghosts don't think xìqǔ schools like them. Girl ghosts drop singing. Raise girl ghosts in Hong Kong. Girl ghosts meet in a tea restaurant with a beauty pageant play set. Porcelain clatters among girl ghost chatters. Girl ghosts want to be the champion. An uncle tells girl ghosts *Champion? More like pork chops!* Girl ghosts tell girl ghosts *Study hard. Compensate for having your father's small eyes!* Girl ghosts take group photos. Swipe other girl ghosts out of the screen. Girl ghosts enlarge themselves in part: Face. Hair. Belly. Girl ghosts suck the eyes out of fish heads with fermented soy beans. The heads of girl ghosts fly out of stuffed winter melons.

Claire Lynn

Live Stream

From different time zones
and latitudes
we are watching the ospreys.
A pip in the speckled shell
of the second egg reveals a membrane
pulsing. In different languages
we are watching the ospreys.
Waiting for the shell
to crack, we remember songs sung
before we were born. We don't deny
the hell-in-a-handcart-going of the world
but we are watching the ospreys.
We count the fish delivered
to the nest each day,
name them trout, flounder, bass
and rate their flappiness.
Watching the ospreys, we revert
to a time long shaken off, cooing
He's such a good provider...
The hatched chicks are all beak.
Their mother passes them
torn-off bits of fish. They eat
and sleep. When dawn breaks
over the Dyfi estuary, we are
watching the ospreys, early risers
in the north-east of England
taking over as the North Americans
go to bed. We gaze at blue skies
over the nest, and we watch storms
roll in, the chicks sheltering
under the umbrella of their mother.
Sometimes we spot a fox
parting the long marsh grasses.

We have wool to spin, exams
to mark, bairns of our own to feed
but we are watching the ospreys –
less than six weeks old
and now as big as their parents.
Do we imagine we have
contributed to this growth with
our watchfulness, our care? Preening
they fill the nest with downy feathers
which blow away like dandelion
clocks. As puzzled as we are
by the preposterous length of their wings
– unfolding angular as music stands –
they stretch them out across a sibling
then stagger to their feet and beat
the air, wind ruffling feathers
not yet primed for flight. Another week
and we are watching them helicopter:
lifting off the nest, hovering, and
clattering back down, not sure
how to detach from the air.
Soon they are flying, from nest
to perch, and on
into the limitless sky. Still
we are watching the ospreys,
blurred specks catching the light
as they soar. Now they can fly
but not yet fish, shouting and fighting
for what their father brings, devouring
everything except the operculum.
Watching the ospreys, we miss their mother,
last seen this morning... yesterday...
last week; gone already when no one
was looking. Perhaps she is crossing
the Pyrenees now, following the same
high passes as the mountain roads.
Safe journey, we murmur, *Godspeed.*

When the weather gets colder
fish swim deeper, out of reach.
Days shorten.
Already the first chick has gone.
She will make the journey to Africa
alone. We watch her younger brother
for signs of the same
mysterious pull of the south...
the south, the south.
His father will wait to watch him set off,
rising, spiralling upwards, rising,
catching the thermals, but we
won't know the ospreys have left
until we realise they haven't
come back.

Nick Makoha

Codex©

When death was a winged horse, I escaped
my country by taking a flight south. Clouds
between the sky and us. Between the earth
and us. I devoted my time to the background
turning slowly as engines roared, en route
to a waiting city. The night seemed to comprehend
and answer, it became a guardian that mistook
me for part of itself. Sometimes it was a gate
or face or a document. But as a desert bird
is silent so was I. As the light turned so did
the stretched wings of the plane. Maybe I'm
only here to wait, the way a mountain waits
for the valley below. The way the future waits
for our lives to take place, learning and watching.

Highly Commended Poems

Gillian Allnutt

Crabapple moon

to Clara, my niece

Bring me my preserving-pan.
It belonged to Gran, *my* Gran.

Tip the washed crabapples in
and water they can boil and bob about in.

They'll simmer until tender
and *we* can wander.

We'll set two chairs upright in the dining-room
back to back with about six feet between them

and lay two tied-together bamboo poles
across the top. Think cross-bar on a bicycle.

We'll set the mixing-bowl upon the milking-stool
between-chairs, in the middle.

Bring me my jelly-bag. That's right, *that's* butter muslin.
Hold it open now and I will tip the tendered apples in,

suspend the bag from the bamboo poles and tie the corners over.
Quietly, under cover

of the coming night, we'll wait for it to drip into the mixing-bowl
upon the milking-stool

and all shall be well
and the moon and the heron, all manner of thing, shall be well.

Mona Arshi

Arrivals

the dead
   how they arrive
in slow trailers

on buses
   the untidy dead
though they carry

no baggage
   they hold
unguarded photographs

and small words
   spoken in
suburban kitchens

or rare marbles
   the colour of citrine
never traded

in childhood
   some wait
by oaken shelters

they exercise such
   tender caution
shoelaces tied

the perfumed dead
   on that long road
the rain spitting from

a sideways direction
    why should there
not be rain

by and by
    and why shouldn't
birds still

stamp for worms
    whilst cat's-eyes blink
in the distance

Bebe Ashley

Sign Language Linguistics

In my first linguistics lesson, I keep stacking
the animals on top of each other in the zoo

in the same enclosure, sharing the same
topographical signing space, the same view.

The Bengal tigers are sunning themselves
between crocodiles in the hippopotamus's pool.

The pandas are preoccupied with the peacock's plumage;
the Alpine ibex are taunting the lazy kangaroos.

Before I point to things, I have to decide
whether they really are where I say they are

so I practise with the planets, and the sun,
stupendous in the centre of the room.

I keep Mercury close to the coffee table,
let Venus and Mars watch over heirlooms,

I fling Jupiter and Saturn onto the lampshade,
let Uranus and Neptune rattle alongside bottles of perfume.

I acknowledge the empty spaces then encounter Earth,
luminous in its orbit of slight ellipticity.

Dzifa Benson

Sestina for Six Scientists in Search of an Ology

The only illustration of a human being in Histoire naturelle des
mammifères *by Étienne Geoffroy Saint-Hilaire and Frédéric Cuvier,
which was otherwise filled with non-human mammals, was '[Espèce
humaine] Femme de race Bochismann' ([Species, Human] Woman of
the Bushman race).*

The woman was Ms Sarah Baartman.

If only her people had eaten men who brought word of God
and savaged anthropologist who tripped across the water.
These men were not contoured human but inferior creations
beetle-browed, drunk on their own sneers, groping in the dark
for Cain's mark, for satyrs and a freckle as giant as the world,
prospecting for sin they tracked *sinus pudoris* to woman.

Man from learned society like physiologist claimed woman
was elbow of the north wind. After him, ethnologist like god,
lips thinner than chimp's, scaled summit of his tiny world,
his creeds bolted on the wing of chimeras, smells in water
poured over the back of her hands to wash away perverse dark
to match paleness of her palms to that of God's real creations.

Phrenologist killed with thoughts to people diorama creations,
climbed prominences of jaws, drilled holes in skulls like woman's,
stored her fragmented body in bell jars, her likeness in rank, dark
liquids, trick mirrors into which he could crisply point to God's
soul as if tenuous links to the blue of veins can be read in water
or a human tail planted in soft ground at sacrum of the world.

Her occiput sitting in well of craniologist's hand, free world
walled in his crude body, he thinks its chambered creations
knows who lives long as trees beside green and fertile waters
and mistakes the red as rooster arteries that mapped woman's

spilled blood for demarcation of empire, land to conquer for God
and country, a border to look at curious flesh through glass dark-ly.

Mouth agape and lantern jawed, gynaecologist, nursed a dark,
deficiency in his eyes. Cold, blind, his speculum as brittle as world
bisected her uterus for her sin – an impolitic bottom – against God.
Pointing to crease in her brain, apishly articulating that creations
from ocean slime to angels don't retain the dust like flayed woman
on account of how her spine tips into coccyx like the flow of water.

Always wounded six-headed hydra still roaming high-tide waters
of her blood vessels and other institutions of uncharted territory. Dark
festering forever caught on the body of always visible, lesser woman
with alleged fixed and innate poverty of blood. As long as a world
of mouths repeats and spreads unknowing, chinless creations
like the white sons of Adam bloat themselves with breath of God.

Six men deigned to walk on all the waters across the known world
and still remain in the light despite their dark sift of the heart of creation
and condemnation of woman who strides on the wrong side of a god.

Alison Binney

Testimony

you have a hole in your
soul your breasts belong to
your future husband we
had a board meeting and
decided that you can no
longer serve you're not as
well-dressed as I thought
you would be that lifestyle
makes me want to take a
shower your life is an
abomination I love you
very much I've stopped shopping at that supermarket that shows two men
cooking lasagne together in their home because I think they're normalising
something disgusting we don't wave flags and hold street parades for proud
burglars maybe if you dressed more feminine and wore lipstick the way you use
love is far from the Christian way you have the theology of a five year old gay
people are the devil's droppings we'd like you to step down from children's
work it might be allowed but it's not God's best life for you my son is a police-
man and those gays are always trying to tell him they're victims and he says it's
so annoying is it possible
you were dropped on your
head at birth Jesus did not
accept everyone when you
celebrate holy communion
it turns into the body and
blood of the devil I have
a duty of care to the
congregation you're only
half a person the way you
live is abhorrent to God
but you're always
welcome if you follow
this path you will live a
very lonely life we love
you and are happy for you
to continue coming to
church but we don't think it
appropriate for you to
speak can I pray for you?

Corinna Board

A dunnock's prayer

O wingless wun,
god o' smæl bridds,
spære my nest,
my fíf blue eggs.
Bright sky-keeper,
bringer o' frost,
maker o' hip an haw,
can ye hear my
tseep tseep tseep
in the hecg?
I sing for ye
in the blackthorn
an the dogrose,
in the hazel
an the rowan.
I, this tyne spearwa
so smæl in yur hand.

Written using a mixture of old English, modern English and phonic variations of modern English.

Pat Boran

Fellow Travellers

The local Traveller camp by the side of the road
is a patch of resistance, history
reduced to a circle of wagons, a tangle
of children and pets, and all the indifferent world
flowing endlessly by. But there was that time,
thirty years back, more, when busking out west
I hitched a lift in a grimy HiAce van,
climbing in from the cold only to clamber up
and over a shifting field of deep-pile rugs
and fitted sheets. Inside, a trio
of teenage girls and an older figure I took
to be their aunt, cross-legged in the gloomy,
oil-smelling dark, and all of them highly amused
by my sudden appearance out of thin air –
amused and, as it happened, unexpectedly shy.
We smiled at each other at first, scarcely speaking
beyond mumbled *howayas* and names, until, outside,
blurred by the curtain of rain and our gathering speed,
the settled and unsettled worlds went hurtling by.

A. V. Bridgwood

Clean Your Plate

       halfway through making him a snack
grandma changed her mind and turned the knife
on him, my dad, that small boy running
down the garden path – no, probably
there was no garden – boy running straight
into the street, terraces crowded like bad
teeth, drunks lying on the doorsteps,
waiting for wives to take them in
with the milk –
       or was it in Southend, they were
always moving – small boy running
past the crouched beach huts, the rotting
nets, running on through the years into this day
of her death, where he's beating the shit out of
the hospital vending machine, trying to dislodge
a Twix, to feed me, from its coil,
unyielding. She's raising
       the knife in the dark 1970s
kitchen, wallpaper fever-orange – no,
60s, it would have been – queasy green
formica, boy in school shorts running
past dads crushing cigarettes on the pier's
rusted girders, small boy running
out into the salt marshes, sinking
through the clinging silt, down and down
into this room where I'm trying to run
and he's blocking the door with the bulk
of himself, where he's 6 foot 4.
       She's raising the knife and he's running
with the plate, balancing the apple slivers,
the white bread with margarine, there
he goes along the shore, tangle
of steel beneath cracked boards, faded

posters for summer shows – or was it summer
then – bright posters, fat gulls, blackened
bones of the pavilion – no, it would have been
before the fire – white bones of the pavilion, loose
slats splintering his boy feet, past horses
grinning on the carousel, coins layered like slate
in the slot machines, further and further
past the great fire in years to come,
past the five-million-pound restoration
after his time, with a boy-leap crashing
through the black eel-muscled water
            out into a future where, long dead, he passes
me the plate and I throw it at the wall,
streak of margarine on the Farrow and Ball,
child I'll never have screaming, husband
I'll never have screaming, enough, enough,
            it stops here.

J. R. Carpenter

Of Nothing

after John Cage

I am here. and there is nothing to say. no whispering. wind in the wych elm. no rumour. of rain. in the river even. the water a rush of nothing I know the language for. and on the far shore. a loose assortment of nothing I know the name of. if among you there is a wish to get somewhere. you may wish. to leave at any moment. if among you there is a murmur. of morning mist. of stone cold. silences. fingers red. and fossilised corals. frozen in time. what cold requires is. that I leave off lecturing. what stone requires is. that that I go on walking. push over a boulder. and the pushed reveals another. an entertainment of the relative significance of marine fossils found in bedrock. as opposed to marine fossils found in cobble. a discussion of the relative knowing of birds identified by song. as opposed to birds identified by sight. I am not opposed to not seeing. song is not silent. even if we are not speaking. stones are not nothing. even if not ocean. and we are now crawling. squint. over cobble covered with sun-cracked. silt. dry creates an absence. nothing produces a surface. and speaks some other language. shall we discuss this later? measure. this whether. we simply decide. the names for these marvels. or agree. to none. to put no name. to know no thing. to refuse. to organise. to lecture on. or in. this space between rain drops. of time between lightning strikes. lecture on whatever you like. there are silences we want to do away with. there are stones that help make silences sink. into nothing. there are silences that let stones think. attach to any one stone any one thought. it falls down easily. I have nothing to say. and I am saying it. and that is poetry. as I need it.

Roberto Salvador Cenciarelli

Footnotes to Untitled (Buffaloes) 1988-89

after David Wojnarowicz and Eric Yip

1

8

2   7

6

3

5

4

---

1. There was a time it wasn't in my awareness, the meat / hanging on hooks off
   14th Street, NYC, the clubs, the sex, the buffaloes

2. falling off the cliff, one by one, how a poet will then write / *the story needs the cliff
   as much as it needs / the buffaloes*, that the cliff could speak, which is to say

3. my ancestors are everywhere in this photograph. David, it took me time to
   learn / how to pronounce your name correctly. In a tape you ask how

4. you dying of AIDS in 1989 is not political, I think of how / our safe spaces
   could only fit among the carcasses of cows, of how

5. after a night of glitter and sweat we would've to expunge the morning / smell of
   bovine blood off our skin in the showers, scrub it like

6. a scratch card. Violence enters us the way a butcher hands / a receipt over the
   counter, a breakdown, bloodied

7. in the margins. The first time I did the test I was twenty: / there were two of us
   in a remote wing of a hospital that

8. echoed at our steps as if frowning upon our bodies. I have seen / the diorama of
   the cliff online, it isn't that tall, meaning

9

10

11

12

13

14

---

9. most buffaloes would've survived

10. with minor injuries. When Marco told me he was positive / over the phone, I wasn't brotherly at all, in fact, I froze

11. fearing for myself that the way we touched each other was final and spent / the next hour in the queue of a helpline only to find my worries

12. lacked education and gauge how quickly I could distance myself from / another man. Buffaloes aren't stupid, they don't jump off cliffs,

13. cliffs aren't cruel nor ignorant, they merely administer gravity. If you want to / understand the story, you ought to put down the camera and

14. expand the picture, colour in the prairies, look for the hunters, see / how they ride, the terror among the buffaloes — admit / the bows and arrows waiting at the bottom of the cliff.

Tim Craven

Sonnet

This reward is just micromoles
of dopamine dripping off
the midbrain floor; axon tentacles
crisscrossing the hemisphere-halves;
the caudate nucleus lit up like Reno.
The cut brakes of obsession from 5-HT
siphoned off in the night and runaway hope
spat loose from the amygdala, beating heart
and quickness of breath
just sympathetic circuitry.
I have the science
but the scent
of your apricot shampoo
is inexplicable, inescapable.

Sasha Debevec-McKenney

Like

As I led the man through
the crowded restaurant
and to his table at the back
he said, "You sure are packing
us in here like on slave ships,"
when he could have said
anything else: packing us in here
like daisies into a grocery-store
bouquet, packed together
like the pages of a wet book,
like A-listers in a Wes Anderson movie,
like hemorrhoid cream in an unopened tube,
like pennies in a pickle jar,
like forty to fifty exuberant,
rural children in an underfunded
classroom, like a family of polar bears
crowded together on a floating sheet of ice—
he could have said, even,
like your ass in those jeans.

Blood in a syringe, silver compact
vehicles on the Beltline at rush hour,
Styrofoam tight in its cardboard box.
Yes, I was packing him in there,
like textured ground-beef material
into a Taco Bell Grilled Stuft Burrito,
like Amish girls in the back of a white van
on the way to Walmart. Like bone regrowing
inside a plaster cast. Like the flames
in a fire, like the fingers in my fist.

Mae Diansangu

Mary Magdalene

Three days before her 86th birthday,
Mary Magdalene re-writes the Bible.
Dedicated to everyone whose survival
has been criminalised.

She deletes every instance where
black represents suffering and death.
Now, darkness is a symbol
of strength, hope and purity.

The gospel of Mary is frothing
with god-slayers and shame-eaters.
Saints in leather, whose bodies burn
with the language of rebel angels
cast out for being too proud.

Mary smiles out loud as she drops
the first draft in the last supper
group chat.

Peter is typing...
Simon is typing...
Peter is typing...
Matthew is typing...

Peter: Let's be honest, Mary. Casting you
in the original was just pandering and virtue
signalling. Now you're shitting on the source
material?! This obsessive need to wokify
everything is EMBARRASSING!! PLEASE STOP!

Matthew is still typing.

God has left the chat.

Mary yawns. For decades, these small men
have tried to abridge her, but she remains
a giant of a woman.

She is canon.
She is the source material.

Mary Magdalene sparks a joint
and concludes her gospel:

> *The good news is, we can save ourselves.*
> *The bad news is, we probably won't.*

Ian Duhig

An Aroko for David Oluwale

1930-1969

Oluwale is Yoruba for 'God has come home'
but he came to find hell in God's Own County,
no home but cold Leeds streets or police cells,
in his asylum only electroconvulsive therapy.

Now by the Aire, where David drowned fleeing
policemen's boots, his feet light from hunger,
my small nomadic cowrie garden grows for one
who'd grown to be a shell of himself in this city.

An empty cowrie is full as an egg with meanings:
Gods' eyes, they make arokos, magic messages.
Because efa, Yoruba for six, has the same letters
as the word to draw, my six cowries set down here

draw David's Christian ghost into Oshun's arms,
water Goddess with a name of water, that he too
might step into the true meaning of his name,
borne back to Africa where the river of us all rose.

This alchemy of cold fire on the Aire's earth makes
nothing happen, like poetry, yet makes something
from nothing for a man treated like he was nothing,
making room to reflect on river water running softly.

Will Eaves

Gold-making

i.m. Simon Adams

Life and work – failure, pain, pleasure – are one.
Invention is not an alteration but a becoming: the transformation
comes before you leave the wings and feel the lights.
Feel it work on your make-up, your costume and character.
You are a Dutch Puritan, a Deacon of Amsterdam, the Anabaptist
  Ananias.
I am Subtle, shaking a flask, looking stage-right into the dark.
You are nobody for a prolonged instant, your body a door
through which the rest of us, the gulls and cozeners, the bawds
and charlatans and underdogs, must pass.

Do as little as possible.
All any of us can do is make a shape with the time we have.
It may be the shape already exists, in which case the making is only
  discovery,
and failure no more than a refusal to see what was always there.
Jesus spoke to Ananias in a vision and told him to go
to the 'street which is called Straight' – *decumanus maximus*, East–
  West
across the old city of Damascus – and ask in the House of Judas for
  Saul of Tarsus.
There Ananias restored Saul's sight and baptised him.
In Acts 22, Paul calls you 'a devout man according to the law'.
You were martyred in Beth Gabra,
beaten 'with a whip made from the tendons of an ox' and stoned.
You were A Faithful Brother.
Fanciful to pretend to remember, but I think
you were reading a book called *A Work of Doubtful Authenticity*
while I rehearsed *A Christmas Carol* and the Berlin Wall came down.
We had no money. I felt you would pursue a modest exaltation.
And now you *are defeated. All the works are flown in fumo, every glass is*

burst.

Or perhaps not. Perhaps *it is only the disease of the unskillful to think
     rude things*
greater than polished, or scattered more numerous than composed.
Stand over there and let the light find you.
Helplessness is necessary.
Out of it comes what you couldn't have been, if you'd been in control.
Art isn't a series of statements. *One at Heidelberg made it.*
The alchemists were mathematicians when they said one form of
     matter
underlay all further expressions.
To find the base matter was surely a kind of factorisation
and gold-making an endless expansion.
Actors double up in character until the fit has passed.
They must accept feelings that aren't theirs.
They put on clothes, habits, encounters, gestures, looks,
wondering how it is that they fit so well and what an intimation of the
     identical
says about people, as if we were merely aspects of each other.

A would-be actor faces in two directions.
At that conjunction we find the decision not to make an entrance
alongside the invisible graft of the person who does.
Both are hidden realisations.
Nothing in life is properly displayed.
The peace of mind rest within these walls.
My thoughts, ambition's relics, are consumed by news of you, faithful
     brother,
who has vanished into acceptance, whose performances were manners.

Josh Ekroy

Benefiting the Publick Pocket

There is no more melancholly Object
than that of the Manufacturer of Bombs
& Bastinadoes during a Time of Peace.
For how is this estimable Worthy
to feed himself when his Emoluments
are precipitately diminished?

It is, therefore, an incontrovertible Principle
that this enterprising Briton must be ever
alert to the *Casus Belli*. There being no Lack
of such in the Levant, it is entirely in Accordance
with Charitable Precepts that Bombs & Bastinadoes
be dropped from a great Height upon the malignant
Philistine, notwithstanding that it is admitted
on all Sides that such a Proceeding is wholly
devoid of Purpose & may do sterling Service
as a Kind of Recruiting Officer to the Enemy
whose desire for Revenge is thus inflamed.

Yet it is wholly desirable, for doth it not afford
Grounds upon which the Manufactury is called
to produce and sell yet more Noxious Weapons,
thus benefiting the Publick Pocket? This, I say,
improves the State of this proud Nation's Health
& Education & is used to prevent the Encroachment
upon these Shores by ill-disposed foreign Persons.

It is not to be thought that when those Weapons
which we have willingly supplied are used
for more nefarious and less easily justifiable Ends,
viz. the bloody Extirpation of newborn Babes,
& the deliberate Imposition of Murrain and Plague,
that we forbid their Sale. Quite the contrary.

Mohammed El-Kurd

Tonight We Die as a Family

At the hospital the nurse is startled
a surprise visitor: her husband's corpse
on a stretcher
he arrived in the backseat of a taxi –
a makeshift hearse.
There are not enough ambulances in Gaza
and more than enough death.
She is livid. *Men never listen*
I told you wait till after my shift
I need to tend to the wounded first
I told you tonight we die as a family
we were supposed to die
as a family

Paul Farley

Turkeys

One with a shock of bollock wattle
and the quick eyes of a Shadow Minister for Agriculture and
    Livestock
pokes its neck in. 'Before we move forward
I for one would like to understand what we're dealing with here.'

One with lobes as red as a Rouge Coco lipstick
raises its head. 'It's called Christmas. It's a human event.'

The Shadow Minister flaps its snood and gobbles. 'We know,
but *what* do we know? We feel the sheds
growing overcrowded and loud, the pecking worse
as the days shorten, but what's the deal with Christmas?'

One enormous Bronze tom weighs in. 'They are celebrating the birth
of their saviour, who was born in a shed too.' The Shadow Minister
blushes, engorged. 'So, all this for a poult?'

'The poult *Jesus*,' answers the Bronze tom, eyeballing nothing
in the shavings then scratching it furiously. Rouge Coco burbles to
    think
of the little poult on starter pellets. The Shadow Minister

turns to the flock. 'And was the poult Jesus slaughtered at twenty-
    four weeks?'

Uproar. Flapping of lobes. *No!* The Shadow Minister
has them. Sideways strut. Flirted fan. 'Let's put it to a vote.'

Vona Groarke

Hindsight

for my brother, Ray

This pipe of light I pull myself through
like a rag through the barrel of a shotgun
to clean it as my father taught me,
unloaded, double-checked, farm gun
spatchcocked on our kitchen table
for the washed-out squares of old
cotton towels and my baby clothes
threaded on a straightened hanger
to be fed in one end and budged all
the way up until out at the muzzle,
two times each barrel, processional,
the rags well-chastened by smut
and grease before I'd flick it,
the shotgun, shut again with a sound
I'd think was like a shot, and lift it,
the shotgun, two hands for the heft,
to carry it over to the tall press
left of the washing machine
and slot it, the shotgun, back between
ironing board and sweeping brush
until the next sign of foxes
in the lambing field but I'd
never see any of that . . .

This pipe of light I pull myself through
is nothing like that one, I suppose,
though my eye is level with its breach
so I can see the last of evening
creep away from the back door.

Bethany Handley

Limbs not walked on

And he informs me a leg is not a leg
if not walked upon; a leg not aiding
standing or walking is just a limb.

I see the air these paralysed limbs
displace, the atoms bouncing away
from skin, knocking against each other

like a Newton's Cradle, limbs last named
hiking up the Nantlle Ridge, feet balanced
on the tooth of folded, titled mudstone.

The limbs of Mynydd Mawr are resting.
The mountain is not waiting to unfold and march
but still it moves, each pebble slowly

slipping. A rain drop shifting silt. Each tree root
burying fingers further between the rock.
Each branch snagging the wind.

A leaf is still a leaf when not clutching a branch,
when a leaf curls and rusts and drops
to the ground, catching dew as if turning to metal.

Soon only the blade and veins of the leaf
remain: a moth held to the sun which welcomes
the light. When the river rises to snatch

the leaf's skeleton, swollen
and bruising with muddy run-off
the water is more gelatinous than flowing
but the river is still a river.

Erica Hesketh

Night feed

Daughter attempting to fall asleep on the breast:
I cherish you as you study the problem

from every angle, hot-cheeked locksmith
carefully coaxing pin after pin,

picking the combination with your whole mouth.
One day you will tip into orgasm

with this same quiet focus. Don't ever change.
Tell your lover, or whoever, exactly

what it is you want – their hair out of the way,
the weight of their warm hands just so.

Ashley Hickson-Lovence

Munster Road

Grenada's Lord Kitchener / London was the place for
you whether they liked it or not / ship docker / door
knocker / hotel dish washer / stacking them Ps like
clean plates / chasing the British dream / Grenada's
Sam Selvon / lonely Londoner but not for long /
donned denim back home so refuse to wear it here /
it's a suit & tie ting soon as your shift ends / go meet a
friend / head west first to your flat in Fulham / looking
smoking while smoking / Grenada's Rudolph Walker /
Love Thy Neighbour / can see what Nanny saw / for
sure / from the top floor / her sharp-dressed saviour
/ devoutly tight-lipped / so much she didn't say /
couldn't admit / hid / before pulling an Irish goodbye
/ leaving you behind / Grenada's Sir Trevor McDonald
/ News at Ten watcher / mechanic / wrestler / lollipop
man / father / fudge-buyer / musician / listen /
Mac Miller said *music is a beautiful thing* / & he was
right / that's why I'm *always* tap tap tapping / fingers
on keyboard / pen to table / TV remote on knee /
air drumming to the beat / listening to bangers &
imagining I'm the frontman / following in your fat
footsteps / yellow-soled & fleshy / ankles bulging /
bulbous & swollen / years of keeping rhythm taking its
toll on your toes / your hypertensive heart / socialising
takes practice & I'm tiring / but still writing & writing
& writing

Hasib Hourani

from *rock flight*

a rock

rubble makes a thing holy because
you go to a place and say
this was worth fighting over
and you are not half wrong

two rocks side by side

eventually the rubble stops counting for all that much
because green grows thick through and over
and you can start lying
we're rebuilding

a handful of rocks laid flat

JANNAH meaning heaven
heaven is full of flowers
the universe is a garden

a pile of rocks

JNAYNAH meaning garden
named as such because you're pretty
close to heaven but not quite there yet

a mound of rocks

JENIN as in the city
it's full of farmland and
if you are from there
your world is a garden

one more rock
right on the top

    if it stays put: a mountain
if it topples over: a dismantling

      4. what warrants a war?
        a. beauty (my dad said this)

my grandparents flee the beauty. it's 1948. they are on foot until they reach the refugee camp in aleppo and then they meet. they have five children and they're all born stateless. myself and most of my cousins are born stateless too refugees by inheritance. we now have five nationalities between us passports that allow us to move and move and move again some more freely than others. none of us have palestinian citizenship. my grandfather fled the living in 2015 my grandmother in 2021 they were my last bloodline that belonged to palestine on paper.

i'm in my twenties with my parents and siblings we are trying to go home just for ten days. we are in a black minivan and i spend three hours in the back seat saying: *i don't get it.* and when i get to jenin i say *i still don't get it.* i reach the camp and i say *you're not doing a very good job at explaining it to me.* and then my sister shows me a video she took somewhere along the drive and it's several minutes long and, because the car was moving so fast, it's just a horizontal blur of green and i say *where was i when this was happening?* but not out loud.

      5. nothing ever really stops existing
        a. this means that nothing ever really stops happening
          i. this means that even when you are not in the
            right place at the right time, you'll still be there
            ١. you are always there

those spiky little balls in mountain grass
splintered into your finger tips
forever pricking every thing you touch

man of stone man of mud man of
slip
remember my body when it leaves
if you are afraid that the last rock will ruin everything
it already has

EMPTY:
meaning something is not occupied. this is on an internet
dictionary but who trusts dictionaries or the internet? and
the more time i spend with words the more i realise that
they do not mean anything at all. a rock is not a rock until
it's thrown.

Amaan Hyder

A Complaint

Did you submit it yet? you asked.
No, I said. I was a junior staff member,
fairly new. I feared the complaint itself
would colour my reputation, possibilities
for promotion. I described my complaint to
other friends and family who found it mundane:
reporting it would change nothing.
When I told you, you said you would
put it online immediately. I made you stop.
We were among a race, the English,
for whom lack of complaint brought respect.
You want invisibility, you said.
Another friend asked me if I wanted revenge.
I needed a salary and, in the future,
a larger salary. *What would you like to be
the outcome of your complaint?*
the form asked. I wrote a poem about it:
one version went through the motions
of the incident; another obliquely referred to it.
There was a sonnet in a crown of sonnets
that concluded, *It is a stream of stops
I progress with, a consciousness of margins,
a movement of halts.* I went home after work,
did calisthenics by the sofa. Every day,
I would see the men who locked their doors
when I was nearby. One day, I saw you
by chance, out in the world. I thought you would
want to talk about it so I did not call out, wave
my arms, distinguish myself from the crowd.

Rosemary Jenkinson

Sham Supermarket, Sandy Row

The English half of the signage
is burnt away to nothing; only the Arabic
survives. Baby aubergines lie
by the smashed frontage, bunches
of withered mint, blackened lemons,
ashen avocados in the windowless remains.

Outside Syrian men are gathering
under the watchful eye of smokers loitering
in the pub doorway across the road.
'I'm not scared,' one man is telling
a journalist, though his face says
otherwise, 'but three years I worked here.'

The shutter is hanging at half-mast as you
lower your head and step onto the wet
mulch of sunflower seeds, roasted corn
and spices, an exotic bogland,
a Persian carpet with pools in the aisles
rippling under a dark dripping ceiling.

Charred pistachios are piled
on the flame-leathered skin of the counter
beneath white plastic stalactites.
You crunch through sugared almonds
while gloved men salvage what they can
from the scorched shelves: warped bottles
of yellow oil, fire-darkened olive jars,
melted cribs of toasted sesame.

You're just leaving when a voice
shouts out behind you, 'Wait!' The owner,
Bashir, runs after you and presses

into your palm a gift saved from the fire,
a cube of malban, a little piece of heaven
for your tongue, and rising through
the stale aftermath of the air,
a hint of fragrance and belonging.

Safa Khatib

Dear Safa

you can go

          anywhere you like

  the same image

          follows you

               like a friend

the dead in blue hats

          pulling severed limbs from a black bag

arranging them

       in rows

  over the floor of the white house…

*

you can go

          anywhere you like

the conditions of perpetual war

               will comfort you

  they shape

        what you may think

                  and when

*

elsewhere, white phosphorus

                              coats the night air

and the news
                    is always the news of your innocence…

don't worry

                         about the blacked-out language

of the documents,

                      the u.s. office of strategic services

translating weltanschauungskrieg
                                  into english in 1941

*

go anywhere you like

        even to the islands
                              of greece

        don't worry

                    when you begin to see agave

kneeling in a camp in lesbos

                  cradling the severed head

of her son

it is all in your head

*

you are one of the good ones

                    you have learned well

that the destruction of life

                            is a requirement

of national security

                    enjoy the expanding canon of english literature

as the u.s. africa command

                            conducts torture in the sahel

*

you are one of the good ones

                            so go anywhere you like

macron, biden, netanyahu, sunak, scholz

                    may appear
                                    like friends

in your cosmopolitan dream

                                    in bloodied suits

        singing to the night air: the solution

of the death camp

        we've tried in the levant –

what will come of it?

        what will come of it?

dove / Chris Kirubi

the weather

like gel it fades in the disarming light,
silicone based, exacting ownership.

cloys to learn, finally, its speech
compressed against wet graphics

secreted by puddles
at pavements dull edge.

there is no reprieve from the sound
of the rattling fountain.

Sarah Lasoye

Good Company

I had not thought in words for so long. I called on friends who let me litter-pick scraps of feeling and call the pile 'work' or at least 'practice'. I circle the mug stains they leave on the counter every morning. The cold drawn up from the floorboards through my feet is a kind of rooting, but there are others. Take the deepest breath you've taken all day. Instead of alive, say ravenous. Imagine this – here on earth, you are crowded into the backseat of a car. You are together and so you defeat capacity. The car becomes whatever you choose to share. It spills over with bodies, wet and luminous, red-blooded embroidery. Imagine this – you take your left hand out of the window and to the ground. You scoop up every white road-marker from the concrete. They grow light, ribboning up and into the air like reverse confetti. Together, you near the horizon. The open flame of every occasion, and in such good company.

Gregory Leadbetter

Elsewhere

I stop the car and turn it out to grass.
The world can find its own way home.
The sun is slant along its shine
and I have stepped into the light inside
the summerland springtide hour, surprised
to find the time still day, a stranger
in this spill of land between two names,
a thin road between two signs, not
knowing what I came to find. Somewhere
not quite become a place. A blown tyre
splayed where someone has mown half
the verge, almost a lawn, though
no one has quite been here. Perhaps
this field is why I came, its sickly
leathern yellowed leaves sprayed with bane
that rusts through every growth. But
that cannot be quite right. Nor the roadkill
with its feathers for a dancer's cap, merry
from the stain of pheasant. No, not that.
The next field, a hedge nearer to the bright
horizon, holds a distant eye to mine.
A hare, too much a wish to hope for until
this moment, brown there, both hunkered
and alert. I stopped, but not for that
until she came between the furrows
into space and took my stare. My car
is gone. No signal on my silent phone.

John Robert Lee

from **XX – Epilogue**

I will lift up my eyes to the hills –
From whence comes my help?
My help comes from the LORD,
Who made heaven and earth.   *– Psalm 121:1,2*

1.
After poems, psalms. And canticles of island pilgrims
passing through self-important harbours, smoke-blue banana
    valleys,
villages lounging at curves of bougainvillea lanes. Faith limns

your life salted by Atlantic trades, fretting with Kwéyòl vyélons,
children gone to hard-rock malls of Kingston and Flatbush.
O – in beloved corner shrines of mango blossom, breadfruit
    palm, almonds' broad oval

leaf, chapels of sidewalks' hasty awnings, confessionals of indignant
minivans, the fuming censer of streets' sulphur speech –
O, at every wary block – His Real Presence, and archangels
    gossiping of His Parousia.
After poems, psalms. And your canticles.

I will lift up my eyes to the hills –

Theresa Lola

Situationship

What are we? you ask.
He says I am . . . and you are . . .
But what are *we* together? you ask.
He says labels irritate his skin;
he needs a patch test first.

But when we reach the shore,
how should others address *us*?
They want to know, too, you say.
He smiles, skates his tongue over teeth.
He says, When that time comes

they will be dazzled by the answer.
And oh! did you know that most ships
are named after women? he asks.
Then hands you a paper boat.
He is a master of gifts.

You cleave to the folds.
This is why when you hear
the roving song of the ocean
you think nothing of it.
Until water barges into your lungs.

You scramble for the top
of the paper boat, but the sides
are steeper than you remember
they tip you back
before you can catch some air.

You call out for your lover,
then realise he never boarded.
He was just the engineer
who made this sinking boat for you.
It even bears your name.

Marianne MacRae

Fox

squashed meat glistens
against an unending
slick of tarmac
a solitary eyeball
lying unhinged
seeks its partner
amongst the debris

the wilting tongue
a pink wing flapping
once lapped
the rippling sheet
of water that searches
the far side of the woods

a fly comes now
to identify the body
lays eggs in folds
of soft midriff
embossed
with tyre tread
cross stitch

John McAuliffe

A Sign

for Jeffrey Wainwright

Nothing's fanciful in their welling up from the black earth,
the mushrooms' little accented cliffs,
pencil shavings the green moss borders and leans on.

Awkward customers on the earth's cold shoulder,
their frills and petalled cairn fester
by the body of water a boardwalk carries us across.

The moving peat was a test to walk, unlike the boardwalk's line,
which I hang on to, wishing it were permanent
as the sprawling fire of winter daylight whose argument

brightens what springs up overnight,
the birch branch suddenly alive in the aspiring woods.
How we labour under its high sign.

Olivia McCannon

Autoemotive Funerals

I

[zombie materialism]

The graveyards of things
are full

The places where things rest
are unrestful

Things do not know how
to say goodbye

II

[scrapyard end-rites]

    when a car dies all the other cars gather round it
and honk
    they want to know why it happened how it
affects them how
    did it die? how does this change the way they
socially stratify?

III

[car-coffin text]

From: *The Book of Motorways*

Ah, Helpless One!
I have found you lying on your side
Did you come on the M5?

Help me out sometimehumes
I have no formula for this committal

You were more to me in your day than
crumpled metal oven-sarcophagus-fridge

You will not decay in the earth
You are corrosive cosmos-fodder
debris over ground under sky

Your petroleum spirit has arrived
at junction 3a of the M6 relief road

but your
toll has not been taken from you

IV

[final breakdown instructions]

Dig trench
Craft chamber
Raise mound
Arrange goods –

Coins ingots bowls
RAC sticker piglet bones
Candelabra carburetor
Antlers spark plugs
Fuel injector

Place
Warning triangle

Put on
Hi-vis vest
Stand well back
at side of road

Clamate on the emergency phone

Ian McDonald

Old Moon

Dull, lopsided rock in the sky,
bruised, rotten-orange tint,
It drops slowly in the black sea,
all its gold and silver travels spent.

Monica Minott

Basquiat's Delusion

I am an apprentice to colour,
to dismantling my father's soul.
I give expression to error: a spider's
web, wind, grey, fog, and hurricanes.

I make it back home before
gangsters come out; splitting
coded colours ain't like hijacking
a parked car, it takes more time.

I learn how to cut the light
shading the sacrifice. Madonna
tied me to the stake. A ram is the
preferred animal. But a goat kid

knows the words I want to say;
I never imagined a world where
fragments could displace bones.
I capture ice splinters in black &

white, a spider eating his prey. I
lay me out in green pastures; they
say I'm delusional because I choose.
I choose to blunt resistance,

to silence rhetoric of sketchy men,
they who'd sideline my prints,
fictionalize my presumptiveness.
I harbour no dread delusion. Life

does not always send good rain.
Sometimes the flood overtakes
the land, calling me out to paint
tsunamis without rainbows.

David Morley

Dialect

Evening froze to a night nailed with stars.
I watched a birdbox fill with flying words
fleeing the chill by bundling in on each other.

I took the box from its hook and prised its lid
and shook the lives of language out of it
festooning my table with wings and feathers,
writhing, fluttering, like a bird made of birds:

Bumbarrel, Hedge Mumruffin, Poke Pudding,
Huggen-Muffin, Juffit, Jack-in-a-Bottle,
Feather Poke, Hedge Jug, Prinpriddle,
Ragamuffin, Billy-featherpoke, Puddneypoke,
Bellringer, Nimble Tailor, French Pie,
Long Pod, Bush Oven, and Miller's Thumb.

I tucked them in this box before they woke.

Theresa Muñoz

Animals

like lions, we raised our heads on the hill
the winter day we wed at Edinburgh Zoo

like swans we paired for life
like squirrels we saved for the winter glut
like peacocks we dressed in high pomp:
purple streaks above my eyes like tiger stripes,
and your silk tie shimmered like an otter's pelt

like meerkats our guests stood in a half-arc
and embraced the noon light, our vows
like parrots we chanted, like elephants we wept
like penguins we nuzzled necks
to the swooping joy of the crowd

like gazelles we raced down a carpet
like rabbits we reached the end and turned round
like monkeys we lifted our palms for rain
you slung your jacket over my shoulders,
it smelled of you completely & fitted like a skin

like honeybees we danced, like hippos we gorged
like pigeons we homed to our sea-facing house
like camels we cast long shadows into the night
and like lions, we lay down

Fawzia Muradali Kane

Namesake

i.m. Fawzia of Egypt
(5.11.1921 – 2.7.2013)

I am not the daughter of a king, or even the sister of one. I was not
given as a contract between countries, to add stature to bandits.

I know the grief of homesickness. My uncle loved me, as yours did,
when he saved your *whisper of a body*, and took you home.

You bartered with your daughter's life. I have nothing for such
an exchange. You discovered that to learn to love is to live. I had that too.

When your sisters fled, you chose to stay with your new love, became a
    stranger
in your own land. There are too many dangers if we remain ourselves.

And if my love also dies before I grow old, where will I walk? Will all
we have built fade into pictures, where we stand sad-faced and silent?

Beyond the decay of shrouds and caskets, lies the grace of caged lives.
May our passing be quick, our bodies washed by women who cry,

the courtyard swept before pallbearers jostle, the muezzin hushed among
all emptiness that remains. Let these be deaths that give light to wonder!

Andrés N. Ordorica

Good Friday

The curtain was pulled back
and at my feet stood the Holy Mother
and Mary Magdalene – two bored girls
the year above me. It was too late.

Neither woman could protect me.
Neither woman could stop the madness.
Neither cared about the pain I held.

For seven minutes, in front of my entire
confirmation class, I stayed standing,
strung up on a large cross, naked to the waist.

How diligently I kept my eyes shut
even when the soldiers, three burly boys
from school, lifted me down, a broken body
caressed by their sinewy arms – whiff of musk and longing.

Oh, how they crucified me, just like they did our Lord,
then how they wrapped me in virgin muslin.
I didn't breathe a single breath – *I swear to you.*
With eyes held shut I let them bury me in the tomb.

If only the crowd knew the truth of who I was . . .
they'd have crucified me a thousand times over;
they'd have lanced me each with their judgements;
they'd have stoned me in verse and dogma and hellfire.

Until all my many coloured lights, all my hidden desires
poured out of me and stained what was once white and pure –
red violent blood and blue silent tears shed upon the rock.

Ness Owen

Naming the Trees

finding the words is another step in learning to see

– Robin Wall Kimmerer

The more I sit with you
the less I'm sure
your leaves tell one story
your bough another.

You speak in layers,
leaf litter,
mor, moder, mull.

How would we capture you
in just one word?

We name you the sound of the wind
in your leaves.
We name you the animal that
you draw near.

We name you bud, flower, fruit.
We name you to keep you alive.
We name you to keep you with us.

Pascale Petit

The River

started to flow when I was thirteen –
it grew between me and my mother.
I saw the jaguar bathe in the shallows.
The caiman with his crown of horseflies
accepted me as a friend.
He led me to the swift centre
where night hawks roosted on driftwood,
raised their sleepy eyelids, and were not
angered by my presence.
They were forest-dreaming
as the current took me in its arms
and whispered encouragement.
My mother's chair seemed further away
on the far bank and I could no longer
hear the words that stung. The river
glittered with waves and each
was a picture I could paint
or a book I could write. It was
as if I'd entered a new element
and could breathe water. My feet
touched the bottom where stones
told me their stories and I listened.
Capybaras barked a welcome
and even the cowbirds on their backs
gurgled as they plucked botflies
from their mounts. I plunged
into the fertile world and swam to safety.
I wrapped each wave around my neck
like a shawl of sunlight.
The anaconda swam with me
and every scale was a make-up mirror
telling me I wasn't ugly.
My brown eyes were not cowshit

but clean as the harpy eagle's,
morphos drank my tears
and fluttered on my lashes –
everywhere I looked I saw my future
was gilded blue. My black hair
mother had cropped to my scalp
grew into ringlets of vines
on which jacamars and tanagers perched.
Marmosets played in the coils and made me laugh.
When I floated on my back,
my breasts were two turtles drying
their shells on a mudbank.
And when the jaguar dived beneath me
and lifted me up into the light
I clung to his back and rode my life.

Ben Rogers

An Uncertain Lake

Tell us about your whereabouts last week, they said. Tell us about your whereabouts earlier today, they said. Tell us about your whereabouts next week, they said. What does next week have to do with it, I said. Planning to leave are you, they said.

Have you been to the mountains, they said. No I haven't, I said. How long haven't you, they said. I haven't at all, I said. What kind of person chooses to live near the mountains but has no interest in them, they said. I like looking at them, I said.

Did you hear what happened in the woods last week, they said. Why do you look uncertain, they said. I don't know what happened in the woods, I said. That's why I was uncertain, I said. We think it's because you aren't certain what to tell us, they said. That's true, I said. Because I have nothing to tell you, I said. It's our job to get you to tell us something, they said. No one knows nothing, they said.

Do you know what *Deschampsia cespitosa* is, they said. Do you know what *Luzula pilosa* is, they said. No, I don't, I said. You don't know much about nature, they said. I don't know Latin, I said. You did it at school, they said. How do you know that, I said. It's in the records, they said.

What do you know about the lake, they said. I know nothing about the lake, I said. You said that quickly, they said. I am certain, I said. No one is that certain, they said. I am, I said. I would remember, I said. So you are saying that unlike everyone else, your memory is perfect, they said. I'm not saying that, I said. You weren't certain about the woods, what makes you certain about this, they said. I have got used to uncertainty, I said.

Richard Scott

Still Life with Silver Cup, Copper Bowl, Spoon, Apples and Hazelnuts

after Jean Baptiste Siméon Chardin, Marcel Proust and Daljit Nagra

for Daljit Nagra

Tangle of vertices – ovoid, hemi-sphere tilting, lolling –
like how there is a knot in my mind, intractable knot

of being groomed. *And sights that disgust you like half-
emptied glasses.* And a delicate queenliness of clinking,

curved shadow of seolfor, solid confection, on his tongue.
The life of the victim is still a creative one: glints, highlights,

I arm myself with these bright particles. Eye-yomp toward
orifices ringing, the wound of a bowl's yawn, stretched

lenticels of an apple's skin breathing and gold. His frontier
of brun cup shadows, pinked! *Still life will, above all, change*

into life in action. Cones reconstruct the cones. Hermetic
hazelnut birthed from suffocating wood to burnish. Copor!

By which I mean: vulnerability alights in me, uncluttered.
The lambent thatched earth. Linseed suspended, consolable.

Diane Seuss

Little Fugue with Jean Seberg and Tupperware

I've tired of them.
Those dishes I learned to cook for love.
Dishes that were not in my nature
but I suppressed my nature.
For love, for love.
What ridiculous things I've done.
I've said big dick when I meant small dick.
And you know? I've tired
of the French New Wave.
Did I ever love Jean-Paul Belmondo?
Now he seems like some trifling prick
I'd have to call into my office
for disrespecting teacher. I'm teacher.
I had no God-given authority.
I had to self-generate it, like God.
At some point, God had to take the leap
to become God.
Those dishes. I carried them in Tupperware
knockoff storage containers. Drove them
miles, through blizzards, for love.
Love, that little wood tick. That tick-in-the-ass.
Say the word enough times inside your head,
it will fall out of its meaning
like a stillborn, plop, into the toilet.
Even Jean Seberg, so intent on her prettiness.
Rocking the short hair.
Trifling waist. Trifling striped dress.
She died of miscarriage-trauma.
Miscarriage-trauma caused by the FBI.
It is better to get over things.
To forget the stupid recipe for fetus-in-a-jar.
So much of cinema, so much of it,
seemed like something I was supposed to like.

I oohed and aahed in all the right places.
A pretense of breathlessness.
But I sat there squirming. Embarrassed by the jump
cuts. The film where the heroine
cuts off her lover's dick and carries it
around with her in a knockoff
Tupperware storage container. God,
I tried to write papers about these things,
but I found no meaning in the meaning.
I'd focus on the little spaces between
the actor's teeth, or that the actress looked like
the empty-faced Jesus-seeking girls back home.
In the end, as he's dying, he tells her
she makes him want to puke.
Yes, sister, many-a-night has ended thusly.

Rachel Spence

8.18pm 3 June 2022 Ludlow

Thermocline days, unplumbed.
At this hour the river a secret, its stories
flotsammed through pollen, feathers, petals
of willowherb. The kingfisher greyed
by dusk though its blueless swoop is still
the sign of healthy water. We could do
with a sign, you and I, as the cormorant dives
to Jurassic time and the mayflies bend
the surface as they rise and land. Just one day
they're allotted yet they're older than dinosaurs.
Einstein found *witchery* in quantum time
but naiads need no occult clock.
We are our own go-between, the water
smooth behind us as if we'd never been.

Arundhathi Subramaniam

This Fruit

We speak of injustice
over fruit

and horseradish cheese
from the farmer's market.

The weather changes around us,
and the light,

and one day, others will sit
as we do,

and remember
ferociously,

argue
fluently,

leap
into oratory,

effortlessly
choric,

awaken
daily

to the primal instinct
for curriculum vitae,

meet countries
with shiny nameplates,

peddlers who convulse
in a hysteria of self-definition,

those whose enemies
are always elsewhere,

who know whom to emancipate,
whom to blame,

one truth, one face,
always one name.

Even after they've eaten
the summer's ripest peach.

Even after they've eaten
all six hundred and thirteen seeds
of this pomegranate.

Christina Thatcher

The Female Rodeo Clown

must protect the rider, lure the bucking bull
from every injured man. When the crowd
needs distracting from blood and bone,
she must crack jokes, start singalongs,
tear off her own clothes.

When the bull returns, she must be savvy,
map its movements: *spinning, sunfishing, breaking
in two*. When the rider jumps to save himself
she'll whip off her bra to wave in the air:

yoo hoo, come and get me!

The bull cannot resist so, as the cowboy shuffles
to safety, the clown leaps in her body-sized barrel,
braces herself for the beast to kick. She prays
horns cannot pierce sheet metal, hopes
her greasepaint is not running in the heat.

Rebecca Watts

The Mainland

Folk on the mainland
are tightytighty.
Folk on the mainland
walk a rope.

No listening on the mainland,
only talking.
To walk while you talk
and to talk while you type.

What use for the mainland?
Polystyrene and mattresses.
Bad juju on the mainland.
Bad eating. Bad faith.

What use for the ocean?
For swallowing questions.
Who when why what NO:
shh shh on the shingle.

Conundrum: how to slip
through the mainland's fingers.
A few who have done this.
A few who have known.

What happens on leaving?
The end of the story.
The start of a new one:
wingbeats, wind.

Biographies of the shortlisted writers

Juana Adcock moved from Monterrey, Mexico to Glasgow when she was twenty-five. 'I struggled a lot with the switch from writing in Spanish to writing in English,' she writes. 'I had to find my voice all over again, and figure out how to situate myself with regard to a different literary landscape and tradition. In this coming and going between languages it is easy to lose oneself and I wouldn't recommend it, but I think it has also made me strong.'

I Sugar the Bones is Adcock's fourth collection, the first to be published by Out-Spoken Press. It explores what it means to cross from one country or language into another. Adcock is currently working towards a PhD in Translation Studies at the University of East Anglia, focusing on the translation of indigenous poets in Latin America; in 2022 she co-edited an anthology of poetry by women from Latin America, and she has translated full collections by Laura Wittner and Hubert Matiúwàa.

Sarah Ghazal Ali came to her love of language via an unusual route. 'My fifth-grade English teacher made us write out dictionary definitions when we misbehaved in class,' she writes. 'The slow meticulousness of that task and the granular level of attention we were asked to pay to individual words made language a source of wonder for me.' Childhood immersion in rhythmic Qur'an recitations and Urdu ghazals helped to deepen her interest in poetry, culminating in the manuscript of her first collection winning the Great Lakes Colleges Association (GLCA) New Writers Award.

Ali is based in Saint Paul, Minnesota, where she works as Assistant Professor of English at Macalester College, and is poetry editor for the magazine *West Branch*.

Abeer Ameer came to poetry 'through the back door', in her words, after taking early retirement from her career as a dentist. Her debut collection, *Inhale/Exile*, was published by Seren and shortlisted for Wales Book of the Year 2022.

'I find myself preferring the candid reports by photojournalists in the occupied territories, rather than the sanitised news reports in mainstream media,' Ameer writes. 'One particular report about the carnage resulting from airstrikes on a block of flats began with the phrase 'They died in their sleep.' Her shortlisted poem, 'at least', grew as a response to the atrocity. She describes it as 'a form of documentation and bearing witness'.

Raymond Antrobus's shortlisted poem arose out of a commission from New York's Guggenheim Museum, inviting d/Deaf poets to respond to items in their collection; Antrobus selected a piece from the Czech painter František Kupka.

'Performance is an important part of my poetry,' Antrobus writes. 'When I started out there was boring and unimaginative gatekeeping between page and stage; the divide was often coded with class and race. I think that has gone some way towards changing and the Forward Prize Performed category is a positive signpost for that change.' Antrobus's debut collection, *The Perseverance*, won the Ted Hughes Award and the Rathbones Folio Prize – the first time the prize was awarded to a work of poetry. His most recent collection is *Signs, Music*.

Isabelle Baafi's debut pamphlet, *Ripe* (ignitionpress, 2020), was a Poetry Book Society Pamphlet Choice; her Forward-shortlisted collection *Chaotic Good* (Faber & Faber, 2025) was also a Poetry Book Society Recommendation. The collection takes as its subject matter the escape from a toxic marriage, and Baafi has described the book's difficult gestation: 'I was wracked with feelings of deep ambivalence, and so translating thoughts and feelings into words seemed almost impossible. At such times, what helped was tapping into my subconscious: writing from dreams and writing first thing in the morning, before my sense of time and place and logic had fully formed.'

Baafi, based in London, is a Ledbury Poetry Critic and an Obsidian Foundation Fellow. Asked about poets she admires, she lists Nuar Alsadir, Jericho Brown, Anne Carson, Vievee Francis, Will Harris, Terrance Hayes, Paige Lewis, Carl Phillips, Shivanee Ramlochan, and Jo Shapcott, among others.

Leo Boix's second collection, *Southernmost*, grew out of a 'sonnet addiction' which took hold shortly after the publication of his first collection, *Ballad of a Happy Immigrant*. When he submitted the manuscript to Sarah Howe, his editor at Chatto, it contained hundreds of sonnets; they refined it down to just one hundred, presenting what Boix describes as 'a wide-ranging vision of Latin America: with voices, histories, flora, fauna, myth, and rupture stacked and in dialogue.'

Boix grew up in Argentina and moved to England to work as a political reporter. In London, he joined a collective of Latin American and Spanish poets called SLAP; at one of their performances he was spotted by Nathalie Teitler, who encouraged him to join the Complete Works mentoring scheme. Now, Boix and Teitler, along with a team of Latinx writers, run their own mentoring scheme called *Un Nuevo Sol*, nurturing the voices of emerging British Latinx poets.

Tom Branfoot's shortlisted poem, 'A Parliament of Jets', grew out of a *Guardian* article about two Palestinian birdwatchers, Mohamad Shuaibi and Saed Shomaly, and the risks involved in birding in the occupied territories. In Branfoot's words, 'the contrast between birds' borderless flight and their surveilled, restricted experience of land was stark. Swifts and swallows had returned and I was on holiday in the Lake District, where American-made F-15 Eagle fighter jets regularly thundered over the Langdale Pikes for military training. I couldn't help but think of Gaza.'

Branfoot organises the More Song reading series in Bradford, and is writer-in-residence at Manchester Cathedral. His debut collection, *Volatile*, is forthcoming from the87press.

Niall Campbell was born and raised on South Uist in the Outer Hebrides, and now lives in Fife, where he edits the magazine *Poetry London*. *The Island in the Sound* is his third collection (all three have been shortlisted for the Forward Prize). 'This book started slowly, after that usual process of re-learning how to write a poem,' explains Campbell. 'I am the same as most poets in that I tend to not write very much in the year after publishing a book. This fallow period is healthy, as when you do start writing again it comes with all the same frustrations and discoveries of starting out anew.'

Campbell's advice to a new poet starting out is to 'balance every contemporary poetry book you read with one written at least fifty or a hundred years ago. I think there's a richness to understanding that these past poets are every bit as much your peers as the other young poets in your life.'

Tim Tim Cheng's debut collection, *The Tattoo Collector*, was published by Nine Arches in 2024, hot on the heels of her pamphlet *Tapping at*

Glass. Her shortlisted poem, 'Girl Ghosts', draws its imagery in part from stories her mother and grandmother told her during the 2020 coronavirus pandemic. 'There is so much more that I don't and won't know... and we can be pretty unreliable, if not delusional, recounting our lives,' she writes. Her poem purposefully makes room for these ambiguities, as 'a source of play; as disruptions to the totalising narratives from the imperial core.'

Catherine-Esther Cowie was born in St Lucia and migrated with her family as a child to Canada and then the USA, where she participated in the Callaloo Creative Writing Workshop. She is also a visual artist, nominated for the *Best of the Net Anthology* in 2023. *Heirloom*, her shortlisted collection, explores the lives of four generations of St Lucian women through monologue, lyric and narrative forms.

'I wanted to explore the rippling effects of trauma: how it could travel from one generation to the next,' writes Cowie. 'I was also interested in memory – what we remember, how we tell those stories of the past and to whom. Should all stories be told? Which stories free us and which stories entrap?'

Bella Cox first got into poetry through attending open mics and slams while at university in Pretoria, South Africa. 'Competing in, and then winning, poetry slams is what first made me feel like a poet,' she writes. When Cox moved to London in 2017, she continued her poetic journey by applying for as many poetry and writing collectives as possible: 'In 2018 I found myself part of The Roundhouse Poetry Collective, Barbican Young Poets, The Writers Room and London Queer Writers Collective! In retrospect, this might have been too many at once, but I had been bitten by the poetry bug and I was determined to hone all my skills.'

The title of her shortlisted poem, 'Sikiliza', means 'listen' in Swahili, which is the dominant language in Kenya, where Cox mainly grew up. 'For me the poem acts as a swinging lantern illuminating the different, sometimes jagged, pieces of my life that have often felt overly-complicated when explaining where I'm from to new people,' she writes. 'Sikiliza' is also the title poem of her debut pamphlet, published by flipped eye in 2023.

Desree was drawn to poetry by 'its power to create meaningful connections.' She writes: 'Finding rooms full of people who resonated with my words offered a kind of affirmation I hadn't experienced before.

It made me feel seen and helped me see others more clearly.' Desree is an alumna of the BORN::FREE writers' collective, the Jerwood Arts | Apples and Snakes Poetry in Performance programme and the Obsidian Foundation, and was poet-in-residence at Glastonbury Festival 2022. Before her shortlisted collection *Altar*, she published a pamphlet with Burning Eye, *I find my strength in simple things*.

Her advice for poets starting out is to not delete anything. 'That line you hate today might be the spark of something brilliant tomorrow. Give yourself permission to be messy; to experiment, and to grow. You might come back to a scribble in a notebook a year from now and think, "Wow. I am a genius."'

Griot Gabriel grew up in Manchester, and his shortlisted poem, 'Where I'm From', celebrates that city, particularly Longsight and Ardwick. 'It highlights both the joys and sorrows of my community,' he writes, 'which seem to resonate deeply with people from various parts of the country – particularly those familiar with – yet proud of – the struggles from which they were birthed.'

Gabriel is founder of The Poetry Place, a Factory International Fellow, and Manchester's 2024 Slam-o-Vision Champion. Asked which writers he most admires, he mentions Nas, Tupac, Ghetts, Yomi Ṣode and George the Poet. In his words, 'their unique ability to story-tell with raw passion, grit and relevance to their social circumstance, make them orators for the people.'

Joshua Idehen is a British-born Nigerian, currently living in Stockholm, where he is well-known on the jazz and electronica scenes. He's collaborated with music producers and artists, including Sons of Kemet, Ludvig Parment, and Daedalus. His first collection, *Songbook: Collected Works*, came out in 2024, and was a Poetry Book Society recommendation.

'Editing is god's gift to writers,' he explains. 'I nip and tuck at a first draft, and then when I practise and get the words into muscle-memory, more pruning happens; finding different ways to express lines.'

Claire Lynn teaches creative writing around Northumberland. Her poems have been placed in the Bridport Prize, the Wasafiri New Writing Prize and the Marsden the Poetry Village Competition, and have appeared in anthologies including *The Nerve* (Virago), the Ver Prize anthology, and *Beyond the Storm: Poems from the Covid-19 Era*, as well as in *The New European*, *The Independent*, and magazines such as *Butcher's Dog*. Her poem 'Sixteen Summers' was commissioned by the Ilkley Literature Festival 2022. In 2023 she won a competition organised by Nexus for National Poetry Day, with her work displayed at Longbenton Metro Station.

Lynn's shortlisted poem, 'Live Stream', was runner-up in the Mslexia Women's Poetry Competition. The poem is a meditation on the passage of time, care and the cycles of life as seen through the watchful eyes of humans observing ospreys.

Nick Makoha's shortlisted poem, 'Codex©', is part of a sequence he describes as fusing 'the technological energy of Basquiat's paintings with the layered introspection of da Vinci's notebooks'. The sequence took root after Makoha viewed da Vinci's *Codex Arundel* at a British Library exhibition.

From 2022 to 2023, Makoha was poet-in-residence at the Institute of Contemporary Arts. His debut collection, *Kingdom of Gravity*, was shortlisted for the Forward Prize for Best First Collection; in 2021, his poem 'Hollywood Africans' won the Poetry London Prize. His advice for poets is to 'read everything, dead and alive; listen to everything: rhythms, jazz, questions, philosophers, shadows, dreams. Then let the poem shift like tectonic plates the murmurings inside you.'

Zoë McWhinney is a BSL and Visual Vernacular poet based in South East London. 'I've always felt VV had the elegant flow and rhythm which are hallmarks of poetry,' she writes, 'except, stylistically, VV does not use the abstract vocabulary that "traditional" BSL poetry plays with and makes use of, and instead leans heavily into classifiers, visual metaphors, rhythm, flow and personifications.'

Her shortlisted poem, 'The Portrait and the Skylight', had its genesis in a commission from the Library of Birmingham for their International Day Against Violence Against Women event. 'I am so thrilled to continue shining even further and bigger with my signing and poetry,' writes McWhinney, 'turning heads and making people challenge themselves to pay attention with their eyes, for the d/Deaf communities which exist alongside and in-between everyone else to find shape of their inner worlds.'

Michael Mullen is a queer poet and spoken-word artist firmly rooted in Glasgow. Their poetry, alternating between Scots and Standard English, explores queerness and working-class identity. Hollie McNish has described *Goonie*, Mullen's shortlisted collection, as 'an essential tribute to life and fight and love and language'.

Mullen was the joint winner of the Edwin Morgan Poetry Award 2023-24, and was runner-up in the Scottish National Slam 2022. They identify their biggest influence as Edwin Morgan. His 'ability to be humorous, serious, whimsical, parochial, universal and always playful and creative with his language,' writes Mullen, 'is something that has always inspired me.' Mullen is currently working on a follow-up collection to *Goonie*, exploring 'the language we use around our own, and other people's, bodies'.

Vidyan Ravinthiran, like Niall Campbell, has been shortlisted for the Forward Prize for all three of his collections: *Grun-tu-Molani*, *The Million-petalled Flower of Being Here*, and now *Avidya*, a Vedic Sanskrit word referring to spiritual ignorance. 'Navigating the conflict between "impulse and form", these poems seek to understand abandoned landscapes and history,' writes Shash Trevett, reviewing the collection for the *Poetry Book Society Summer Bulletin*. 'Yet this is not a work of diasporan poetry: in *Avidya*, Ravinthiran is as much a part of "there" as he is of "here".'

Ravinthiran is also a literary critic who teaches at Harvard and whose critical works include *Elizabeth Bishop's Prosaic* (2015), *Spontaneity and Form in Modern Prose* (2020) and *Worlds Woven Together* (2022).

Karen Solie grew up on a farm in southwest Saskatchewan and currently teaches creative writing at the University of St Andrews. Reviewing her selected poems, *The Living Option*, in the *London Review of Books*, Michael Hofmann described her poetry as writing which 'seems out of control, but isn't; it exhibits grace while falling, which is perhaps what grace is.'

Wellwater is Solie's sixth collection. 'It certainly has things in common with my earlier work, stylistically and in terms of subject,' she writes. 'But there are changes, too, as I've changed. As you get older, you lose people and that alters you. Your relationship to your voice changes, for one thing, and that influences technical choices. The book is to some extent about mourning, and how the line between elegy and ode is very fine, if a line exists at all.'

Publisher acknowledgements

Juana Adcock · In Springfield, Mexico, Lisa Simpson Speaks in Spanish ·
    After Banksy (Everybody Wanted to Buy a Plot of Land in Paradise) ·
    I Sugar the Bones · Out-Spoken Press
Sarah Ghazal Ali · Story of the Cranes · The Guest · *Theophanies* · the87press
Gillian Allnutt · Crabapple moon · *Lode* · Bloodaxe Books
Abeer Ameer · at least · *MODRON Magazine*
Mona Arshi · Arrivals · *Mouth* · Chatto & Windus
Bebe Ashley · Sign Language Linguistics · *Harbour Doubts* · Banshee Press
Isabelle Baafi · Anti-Hero · The Butterfly Effect · *Chaotic Good* ·
    Faber & Faber
Dzifa Benson · Sestina for Six Scientists in Search of an Ology · *Monster* ·
    Bloodaxe Books
Alison Binney · Testimony · *The Opposite of Swedish Death Cleaning* · Seren
Corinna Board · A dunnock's prayer · *Carmen et Error*
Leo Boix · Sonnet 36 · Sonnet 74 · *Southernmost: Sonnets* · Chatto & Windus
Pat Boran · Fellow Travellers · *Hedge School* · Dedalus Press
Tom Branfoot · A Parliament of Jets · *Ambient Receiver*
A. V. Bridgwood · Clean Your Plate · Oxford Poetry Prize
Niall Campbell · A Man Carrying His Own Door · The Cockle-picker ·
    The Island in the Sound · Bloodaxe Books
J. R. Carpenter · Of Nothing · *Measures of Weather* · Shearsman Books
Roberto Salvador Cenciarelli · Footnotes to Untitled (Buffaloes) 1988-
    89 · VERVE Poetry Festival Annual Competition 2025
Tim Tim Cheng · Girl Ghosts · *Perverse Magazine*
Catherine-Esther Cowie · Mimorian · What I Know · *Heirloom* · Carcanet
Tim Craven · Sonnet · *Good Sons* · Blue Diode Press
Sasha Debevec-McKenney · Like · *Joy Is My Middle Name* ·
    Fitzcarraldo Editions
Desree · The Notorious B.I.G. and Jesus Christ on a Boat · Kim K Takes
    a Photo of Sarah Baartman to Her Surgeon · *Altar* · Bad Betty
Mae Diansangu · Mary Magdalene · *Bloodsongs* · Tapsalteerie
Ian Duhig · An Aroko for David Oluwale · *An Arbitrary Light Bulb* · Picador
Will Eaves · Gold-making · *Invasion of the Polyhedrons* · CB Editions
Josh Ekroy · Benefiting the Publick Pocket · Ver Poets Open Competition
Mohammed El-Kurd · Tonight We Die as a Family · *The Poetry Review*

Paul Farley · Turkeys · *When It Rained for a Million Years* · Picador

Griot Gabriel · Where I'm From · Manchester UNESCO City of
Literature Slamvision

Vona Groarke · Hindsight · *Infinity Pool* · The Gallery Press

Bethany Handley · Limbs not walked on · *Poetry Wales*

Erica Hesketh · Night feed · *In the Lily Room* · Nine Arches Press

Ashley Hickson-Lovence · Munster Road · *Why I Am Not a Bus Driver* ·
Bad Betty

Hasib Hourani · *rock flight* · Prototype

Amaan Hyder · A Complaint · *Self-Portrait With Family* · Nine Arches Press

Joshua Idehen · The World According to Your Mum Doing the Washing ·
Bad Betty · Filmed by I Am Loud for Joshua

Rosemary Jenkinson · Sham Supermarket, Sandy Row · *Sandy Row Riots* ·
Arlen House

Safa Khatib · Dear Safa · *A Dress of Locusts* · Bloomsbury Poetry

dove / Chris Kirubi · the weather · *WILDPLASSEN* · the87press

Sarah Lasoye · Good Company · *And Other Poems*

Gregory Leadbetter · Elsewhere · *The Infernal Garden* · Nine Arches Press

John Robert Lee · XX - Epilogue · *After Poems, Psalms* · Peepal Tree Press

Theresa Lola · Situationship · *Ceremony for the Nameless* · Penguin Books

Claire Lynn · Live Stream · Mslexia Women's Poetry Competition

Marianne MacRae · Fox · *Recital* · Blue Diode Press

Nick Makoha · Codex© · *bath magg*

John McAuliffe · A Sign · *National Theatre* · The Gallery Press

Olivia McCannon · Autoemotive Funerals · *The Lives of Z* ·
Pavilion Poetry, Liverpool University Press

Ian McDonald · Old Moon · *Chasing the Marbleu* · Peepal Tree Press

Monica Minott · Basquiat's Delusion · *Wandering Spirits of Exile* ·
Peepal Tree Press

David Morley · Dialect · *Passion* · Carcanet

Michael Mullen · He Loved Lilies · Tinamints · *Goonie* · Little, Brown
Book Group / Corsair

Theresa Muñoz · Animals · *Archivum* · Pavilion Poetry,
Liverpool University Press

Fawzia Muradali Kane · Namesake · *Guaracara* · Carcanet

Andrés N. Ordorica · Good Friday · *Holy Boys* · Birlinn

Ness Owen · Naming the Trees · *Naming the Trees* · Arachne Press

Pascale Petit · The River · *Beast* · Bloodaxe Books

Vidyan Ravinthiran · Autumn · As a child · *Avidya* · Bloodaxe Books

Ben Rogers · An Uncertain Lake · *Lighthouse Literary Journal*

Richard Scott · Still Life with Silver Cup, Copper Bowl, Spoon, Apples and Hazelnuts · *That Broke into Shining Crystals* · Faber & Faber

Diane Seuss · Little Fugue with Jean Seberg and Tupperware · *Modern Poetry* · Fitzcarraldo Editions

Karen Solie · That Which Was Learned in Youth Is Always Most Familiar · Red Spring · *Wellwater* · Picador

Rachel Spence · 8.18pm 3 June 2022 Ludlow · *Daughter of the Sun* · The Emma Press

Arundhathi Subramaniam · This Fruit · *The Gallery of Upside Down Women* · Bloodaxe Books

Christina Thatcher · The Female Rodeo Clown · *Breaking a Mare* · Parthian Books

Rebecca Watts · The Mainland · *The Face in the Well* · Carcanet

Winners of the Forward Prizes

Best Collection

2024 · Victoria Chang · *With My Back to the World* · Corsair

2023 · Jason Allen-Paisant · *Self-Portrait as Othello* · Carcanet

2022 · Kim Moore · *All the Men I Never Married* · Seren

2021 · Luke Kennard · *Notes on the Sonnets* · Penned in the Margins

2020 · Caroline Bird · *The Air Year* · Carcanet

2019 · Fiona Benson · *Vertigo & Ghost* · Jonathan Cape

2018 · Danez Smith · *Don't Call Us Dead* · Chatto & Windus

2017 · Sinéad Morrissey · *On Balance* · Carcanet

2016 · Vahni Capildeo · *Measures of Expatriation* · Carcanet

2015 · Claudia Rankine · *Citizen: An American Lyric* · Penguin Books

2014 · Kei Miller · *The Cartographer Tries to Map a Way to Zion* · Carcanet

2013 · Michael Symmons Roberts · *Drysalter* · Jonathan Cape

2012 · Jorie Graham · *PLACE* · Carcanet

2011 · John Burnside · *Black Cat Bone* · Jonathan Cape

2010 · Seamus Heaney · *Human Chain* · Faber & Faber

2009 · Don Paterson · *Rain* · Faber & Faber

2008 · Mick Imlah · *The Lost Leader* · Faber & Faber

2007 · Sean O'Brien · *The Drowned Book* · Picador

2006 · Robin Robertson · *Swithering* · Picador

2005 · David Harsent · *Legion* · Faber & Faber

2004 · Kathleen Jamie · *The Tree House* · Picador

2003 · Ciaran Carson · *Breaking News* · The Gallery Press

2002 · Peter Porter · *Max is Missing* · Picador

2001 · Sean O'Brien · *Downriver* · Picador

2000 · Michael Donaghy · *Conjure* · Picador

1999 · Jo Shapcott · *My Life Asleep* · OUP

1998 · Ted Hughes · *Birthday Letters* · Faber & Faber

1997 · Jamie McKendrick · *The Marble Fly* · OUP

1996 · John Fuller · *Stones and Fires* · Chatto & Windus

1995 · Sean O'Brien · *Ghost Train* · OUP

1994 · Alan Jenkins · *Harm* · Chatto & Windus

1993 · Carol Ann Duffy · *Mean Time* · Anvil Press

1992 · Thom Gunn · *The Man with Night Sweats* · Faber & Faber

Best First Collection

2024 · Marjorie Lotfi · *The Wrong Person to Ask* · Bloodaxe Books

2023 · Momtaza Mehri · *Bad Diaspora Poems* · Jonathan Cape

2022 · Stephanie Sy-Quia · *Amnion* · Granta

2021 · Caleb Femi · *Poor* · Penguin Books

2020 · Will Harris · *Rendang* · Granta

2019 · Stephen Sexton · *If All the World and Love Were Young* ·
Penguin Books

2018 · Phoebe Power · *Shrines of Upper Austria* · Carcanet

2017 · Ocean Vuong · *Night Sky with Exit Wounds* · Jonathan Cape

2016 · Tiphanie Yanique · *Wife* · Peepal Tree Press

2015 · Mona Arshi · *Small Hands* · Pavilion Poetry,
Liverpool University Press

2014 · Liz Berry · *Black Country* · Chatto & Windus

2013 · Emily Berry · *Dear Boy* · Faber & Faber

2012 · Sam Riviere · *81 Austerities* · Faber & Faber

2011 · Rachael Boast · *Sidereal* · Picador

2010 · Hilary Menos · *Berg* · Seren

2009 · Emma Jones · *The Striped World* · Faber & Faber

2008 · Kathryn Simmonds · *Sunday at the Skin Launderette* · Seren

2007 · Daljit Nagra · *Look We Have Coming to Dover!* · Faber & Faber

2006 · Tishani Doshi · *Countries of the Body* · Aark Arts

2005 · Helen Farish · *Intimates* · Jonathan Cape

2004 · Leontia Flynn · *These Days* · Jonathan Cape

2003 · AB Jackson · *Fire Stations* · Anvil Press

2002 · Tom French · *Touching the Bones* · The Gallery Press

2001 · John Stammers · *Panoramic Lounge-Bar* · Picador

2000 · Andrew Waterhouse · *In* · The Rialto

1999 · Nick Drake · *The Man in the White Suit* · Bloodaxe Books

1998 · Paul Farley · *The Boy from the Chemist is Here to See You* ·
Picador

1997 · Robin Robertson · *A Painted Field* · Picador

1996 · Kate Clanchy · *Slattern* · Chatto & Windus

1995 · Jane Duran · *Breathe Now, Breathe* · Enitharmon

1994 · Kwame Dawes · *Progeny of Air* · Peepal Tree Press

1993 · Don Paterson · *Nil Nil* · Faber & Faber

1992 · Simon Armitage · *Kid* · Faber & Faber

Best Single Poem – Performed

2024 · Leyla Josephine · Dear John Berger

2023 · Bohdan Piasecki · Almost Certainly

Best Single Poem – Written

2024 · Cindy Juyoung Ok · Ward of One · *Poetry London*

2023 · Malika Booker · Libation · *The Poetry Review*

2022 · Nick Laird · Up Late · *Granta*

2021 · Nicole Sealey · Pages 22–29, *an excerpt from* The Ferguson
   Report: An Erasure · *Poetry London*

2020 · Malika Booker · The Little Miracles · *Magma Poetry*

2019 · Parwana Fayyaz · Forty Names · *PN Review*

2018 · Liz Berry · The Republic of Motherhood · *Granta*

2017 · Ian Patterson · The Plenty of Nothing · *PN Review*

2016 · Sasha Dugdale · Joy · *PN Review*

2015 · Claire Harman · The Mighty Hudson · *Times Literary Supplement*

2014 · Stephen Santus · In a Restaurant · The Bridport Prize

2013 · Nick MacKinnon · The Metric System · *The Warwick Review*

2012 · Denise Riley · A Part Song · *London Review of Books*

2011 · RF Langley · To a Nightingale · *London Review of Books*

2010 · Julia Copus · An Easy Passage · *Magma*

2009 · Robin Robertson · At Roane Head · *London Review of Books*

2008 · Don Paterson · Love Poem for Natalie 'Tusja' Beridze ·
   The Poetry Review

2007 · Alice Oswald · Dunt · *Poetry London*

2006 · Sean O'Brien · Fantasia on a Theme of James Wright · *The Poetry Review*

2005 · Paul Farley · Liverpool Disappears for a Billionth of a Second ·
   The North

2004 · Daljit Nagra · Look We Have Coming to Dover! · *The Poetry Review*

2003 · Robert Minhinnick · The Fox in the Museum of Wales · *Poetry London*

2002 · Medbh McGuckian · She Is in the Past, She Has This Grace · *The Shop*

2001 · Ian Duhig · The Lammas Hireling · National Poetry Competition

2000 · Tessa Biddington · The Death of Descartes · The Bridport Prize

1999 · Robert Minhinnick · Twenty-five Laments for Iraq · *PN Review*

1998 · Sheenagh Pugh · Envying Owen Beattie · *New Welsh Review*

1997 · Lavinia Greenlaw · A World Where News Travelled Slowly ·
   Times Literary Supplement

1996 · Kathleen Jamie · The Graduates · *Times Literary Supplement*
1995 · Jenny Joseph · In Honour of Love · *The Rialto*
1994 · Iain Crichton Smith · Autumn · *PN Review*
1993 · Vicki Feaver · Judith · *Independent on Sunday*
1992 · Jackie Kay · Black Bottom · Bloodaxe Books

Supporting poetry with Forward

Proceeds from the sale of this book benefit Forward Arts Foundation, the charity behind National Poetry Day and the Forward Prizes. We celebrate the best new poetry in the UK and Ireland, and create opportunities for everyone to discover the wonder and connection that only poetry can give.

We fundraise every year from scratch to do what we do, and rely on your support, so thank you for buying this book.

Maybe you remember loving poetry in school. Perhaps now you put pen to paper when nothing else will cut it. Whatever your own reasons for loving poetry, please consider donating to share the love with others.

To find out more, visit our website forwardartsfoundation.org and follow us on Facebook, X or Instagram @ForwardPrizes.

Donate

Scan the QR code to make a donation to Forward Arts Foundation.